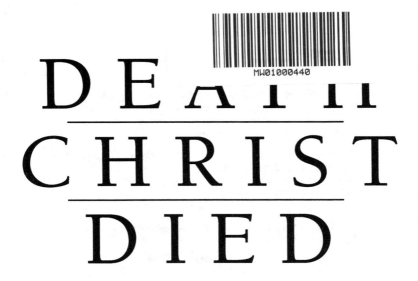

DEATH
CHRIST
DIED

A Biblical Case for Unlimited Atonement

Robert P. Lightner

kregel
PUBLICATIONS

Grand Rapids, MI 49501

The Death Christ Died: A Biblical Case for Unlimited Atonement

Published by Kregel Publications, a division of Kregel, Inc., P.O. Box 2607, Grand Rapids, MI 49501. Kregel Publications provides trusted, biblical publications for Christian growth and service. Your comments and suggestions are valued.

For more information about Kregel Publications, visit our web site at http://www.kregel.com.

Cover photo: © CLEO Freelance Photography
Cover design: Nicholas G. Richardson

Library of Congress Cataloging-in-Publication Data
Lightner, Robert Paul.
    The death Christ died: a biblical case for unlimited atonement / by Robert P. Lightner.—2nd ed.
        p.   cm.
    Includes bibliographical references and index.
    1. Atonement. I. Title.
BT267.L54   1998   232'.3—dc21   98-39124
                                                      CIP

ISBN 0-8254-3155-7

Printed in the United States of America

1 2 3 / 04 03 02 01 00 99 98

To Dr. John R. Dunkin,
whose conviction of unlimited atonement
first stimulated my thinking on the subject

CONTENTS

FOREWORD

This book is a long overdue update of one of the best books written in our generation on the topic of the extent of Christ's death. In recent years there has been a revival of Reformed theology. This is largely due, I think, to reading too much of the Puritans and too little of Paul—and Peter and John.

Some very popular speakers, including J. I. Packer, John McArthur, and R. C. Sproul, have offered persuasive discourses on their Calvinistic view of limited atonement. In this they are obviously more "Calvinistic" than John Calvin, who said clearly and repeatedly of Christ that "he suffered and died for the salvation of the human race" (Institutes 3.1.1). Calvin added, "He [Paul] says that this redemption was procured by the blood of Christ, for by the sacrifice of His death all the sins of the world have been expiated" (Comments on Col. 1:15).

Dr. Lightner, following the plain meaning of numerous Scriptures rather than a preconceived theological structure, calls the church back to its historic belief that Christ "is the propitiation for our sins; and not for ours only, but also for those of the whole world" (1 John 2:2).

By careful analysis of Scripture, an undertaking seasoned with a lifetime of teaching experience, Lightner presents a definitive statement on the extent of Christ's death. He died not just for the elect, but He "gave Himself as a ransom for all" (1 Tim. 2:6).

Having watched carefully the current trend to limit God's love and saving work to a select few (the elect) on whom God works irresistibly apart from their choice, I am convinced that this will be the forerunner of a new universalism. For if God can so effect salvation on some against their will, then why should He not do it to all? The honest answer must be that God does not love all. So much for John 3:16 and the gospel of God's universal love. This would not be the first time this has happened in our country. After all, Unitarianism and universalism grew in the soil of Puritanism.

As Lightner astutely observes, what one believes on this matter also has serious practical implications for evangelism and missions. Without a belief that Christ is "the Lamb of God who takes away the sin of the world" (John 1:29), the gospel cannot be personalized for the sinner. Limiting the atonement to the elect blunts the invitation of the gospel to all sinners and hinders evangelism.

It is my hope that a wide and careful reading of this important work by a noted scholar will occasion a return to the biblical teaching that God "wants all men to be saved and to come to a knowledge of the truth" (1 Tim. 2:4).

In this revised and updated version of Dr. Lightner's landmark work, *The Death Christ Died,* he has done a great service for the church, both theologically and practically. It is my prayer that the church will take heed.

Norman L. Geisler
President, Southern Evangelical Seminary

PREFACE TO THE SECOND EDITION

Long before the first edition of this book was published in 1967, evangelicals debated the questions, "For whom did Christ die?" and "What exactly is the extent of the atoning death of our Lord Jesus Christ?" Early in the history of the Christian church, a number of theories of the atonement were set forth regarding the *nature* of the atonement. These theories sought to answer the question, "Why did Christ die?" rather than "For whom did Christ die?"

The extent of the atonement was not much of an issue until the sixteenth-century Reformation. Up until that time, the prevailing and mostly undisputed view of Christ's death was that it was a provisionary sacrifice for all of humankind, salvific only for those who believed.

The first edition of this volume and subsequent publications received a warm reception and engendered good response among God's people. It has been out of print for a number of years. Kregel Publications, under the editorial direction of Dennis Hillman, has graciously undertaken the publication of this revised edition.

"Man of Sorrows!" what a name
For the Son of God who came
Ruined sinners to reclaim!
Hallelujah! what a Savior!

Guilty, vile and helpless we,
Spotless Lamb of God was He;
"Full atonement!" can it be?
Hallelujah! what a Savior!

"Lifted up" was He to die,
"It is finished," was His cry;
Now in heav'n exalted high;
Hallelujah! what a Savior!

When He comes, our glorious King,
All His ransomed home to bring,
Then anew this song we'll sing:
Hallelujah! what a Savior!

—P. P. Bliss

INTRODUCTION

Whether Christ died for all men or for only those who will believe has been an issue much debated since the days of the Reformation. Prior to that time much was written about the nature of the atonement but very little about its extent. Some older writers insist, however, that the church from its earliest ages was of the opinion that Christ died for all. Even Augustine, strict predestinarian though he was, maintained that Christ gave Himself a ransom for all by providing for their salvation, thus removing an impediment which would otherwise have proved fatal.[1]

There are scattered indications in the writings of some of the early fathers which certainly imply their belief in an unlimited atonement. Of course, it must be remembered that their first concern was not with the extent of the atonement but with the person of Christ and with the nature of His work on the cross.

Irenaeus, who lived about A.D. 130-202, wrote a treatise entitled *Against Heresies* in which he challenged some of the heretical groups springing up in the church. Speaking of Christ and His work on the cross, he said that He ". . . gave Himself as a redemption *for those who had been led into captivity* [italics mine]."[2]

Another such strong hint by an early writer of the universal scope of Christ's provision at Calvary comes from Athanasius, staunch defender of the faith, who lived and labored from A.D. 298 to 373. In his work, *The Incarnation of the Word of God,* he makes the following observation concerning Christ's humanity and death. "Thus, taking a body like our own, because all our bodies were liable to the corruption of death, He surrendered His body to *death instead of all,* and offered it to the Father [italics mine]."[3] Again, the same writer said: "Death there

---

[1] James Richards, *Lectures on Mental Philosophy and Theology* (New York: M. W. Dodd, 1846), p. 302.

[2] Robert L. Ferm, *Readings in the History of Christian Thought* (New York: Holt, Rinehart and Winston, Inc., 1964), p. 186.

[3] *Ibid.,* p. 193.

had to be, and *death for all,* so that the due of all might be paid [italics mine]."[4]

As far as the great ecumenical councils of the ancient church are concerned, there is nothing in their pronouncements which would militate against an unlimited atonement. In fact there are statements in the creeds, which followed the councils, which strongly imply belief in the unlimited view. For example, the sixth council in Constantinople (680-681) declared, "Wherefore we confess two wills and two operations, concurring most fitly in him for the salvation of the human race."[5] Statements similar to this can be found in most of the councils' pronouncements.

Statements such as these and similar ones in the writings of the early church have led some to believe that from the beginning of the Christian era Christ's death was viewed as a true and perfect sacrifice for the sins of the elect and the nonelect. This sacrifice, they maintained, was provisionary in nature and became effectual only to those who trusted Christ as Savior.

"But even all this does not suppose that the death of Christ, considered simply as a *sacrifice for sin,* had anything in it peculiar to the elect, or that in and of itself it did anything for them which it did not do for the rest of mankind. The intention of God, as to its application, or the use he designed to make of it, is a thing perfectly distinct from the sacrifice itself, and so considered, as we believe by the church antecedent to the Reformation. In no other way can we see how their language is either *intelligible* or *consistent.*"[6]

The reformers, and certainly the children of the reformers, were not united on this matter. It is, of course, no secret to the student of the Reformation that the Lutheran branch almost without exception embraced the unlimited view. "But that Luther, Melanchthon, Osiander, Brentius, Oecolampadius, Zwinglius and Bucer held the doctrine of a general atonement there is no reason to doubt. . . . Thus also, it was with their immediate successors, as the language of the Psalgrave Confes-

---

[4] *Ibid.,* p. 196.
[5] *Ibid.,* p. 181.
[6] Richards, *op. cit.,* p. 304.

sion testifies. . . . 'Of the power and death of Christ, believe we,' say these German Christians, that the death of Christ (whilst he being not a bare man, but the Son of God, died,) *is a full, all-sufficient* payment, not only for our sins but for the sins of the whole world. . . ."[7]

The Heidelberg Catechism (1563) of the German Reformed Church in answer to the thirty-seventh question, "What dost thou understand by the word *Suffered?*" has this answer: "That all the time he lived on earth, but especially at the end of his life, he bore, in body and soul, the wrath of God against the sin of the whole human race. . . ."[8]

The Church of England's official statement of faith is equally clear in its embrace of unlimited atonement. Article thirty-one of The Thirty-Nine Articles reads: "The offering of Christ once made is *that* perfect redemption, propitiation, and satisfaction, for all the sins of the whole world, both original and actual; and there is none other satisfaction for sin, but that alone."[9]

Those who believe in limited atonement usually assume that John Calvin's writings set forth clearly the limited view. This assumption may be open to some question, however, since on at least some occasions he presents his views in such a way as to make one think he is carefully avoiding the issue. In his *Institutes of the Christian Religion,* which were written early in his life, one gets the impression that he does not commit himself on the matter. His language there is in keeping with the language generally adopted by the church of his day, which was not very specific regarding the extent of the atonement but favored an unlimited concept.

During the later years of his life Calvin wrote his commentaries, which reveal some development of thought, and in which he avoided some of the extremes found in the *Institutes.* This every honest student of Calvin will readily admit. Some believe without any hesitation that in his commentaries Calvin taught an unlimited atonement. "But whatever might have been

[7] *Ibid.,* pp. 304, 305.
[8] Philip Schaff, *The Creeds of Christendom* (New York: Harper & Brothers, 1877), p. 319.
[9] *Ibid.,* p. 507.

his opinions in early life, his commentaries, which were the labors of his riper years, demonstrate in the most unequivocal manner that he received and taught the doctrine of a *general* or *universal* atonement."[10]

Whether that be true or not, it is true that Calvin's comments on some of the most controverted passages make one hesitant to assign him the role of a limited redemptionist. For example, on John 3:16, he said: ". . . The Heavenly Father loves the human race, and wishes that they should not perish."[11] Concerning the term *whosoever* in the same verse, he said: "And he has employed the universal term *whosoever,* both to invite all indiscriminately to partake of life, and to cut off every excuse from unbelievers. Such is also the impact of the term *world,* which he formerly used; for though nothing will be found in *the world* that is worthy of the favour of God, yet he shows himself to be reconciled to the whole world, when he invites all men without exception to the faith of Christ, which is nothing else than an entrance into life."[12] Such an understanding of this verse and the words employed in it is certainly not in keeping with many who claim to be Calvinists, as the following pages will reveal.

Another illustration of Calvin's view is to be found in his explanation of Matthew 26:28: ". . . This is my blood of the new testament, which is shed for *many* for the remission of sins [italics mine]." He says: "Under the name of *many* he designates not a part of the world only, but the whole human race."[13]

The citations from early church fathers, the creeds and confessions, and John Calvin have not been given as arguments in favor of unlimited atonement. They have been cited, though, to demonstrate that the unlimited view is not new; nor did it originate with Arminianism. The fact is, the limited view was not popularly held until the formulation of the canons of the Synod of Dort (1619) and the Westminster Confession of Faith (1647).

Throughout this work I have used the words "atonement"

---

[10] Richards, *op. cit.,* p. 308.
[11] John Calvin, *Commentary on the Gospel According to John* (Grand Rapids: Wm. B. Eerdmans Publishing Co., 1949), I, p. 123.
[12] *Ibid.,* p. 125.
[13] John Calvin, cited by Richards, *loc. cit.*

and "redemption" interchangeably. Some may object to this on the basis that redemption, it is contended, relates only to the believer and ought never be used in any sense of the nonbeliever. However, there are instances in Scripture where the word "redeem" or its cognates are used of Christ-rejectors. The best example of such a usage is found in 2 Peter 2:1 (cf. Gal. 4:4, 5). Therefore, since the word "atonement" has come to refer to the totality of the completed work of Christ, and since redemption is used of both saved and unsaved, we have used them both when speaking of Christ's work on the cross. It is readily admitted, of course, that no one benefits from that purchased redemption until he believes in Christ as his Redeemer.

This subject is of paramount importance to the ambassador for Christ. Unless Christ died for all men, the message of God's love and Christ's death must be given with tongue in cheek and with some reservation, because some may hear who are really not to be numbered among those whom God loved and for whom Christ died. Consistency and honesty would demand that the one who believes in limited atonement refrain from proclaiming God's universal offer of the good news of God's love and grace in Christ to all men indiscriminately, since in that view God did not extend grace to all nor did Christ die for all. Therefore, to tell all men that these things are true and that salvation is available for them is to speak that which is not true if the limited view be accepted.

It is hoped that this study will enhance the cause of Christ, stimulate a deeper interest in personal Bible study, and give every confidence and assurance to the proclaimer of the gospel that without reservation or hesitation he can tell all men that Christ died for them according to the Scriptures.

One day when heaven was filled with His praises,
One day when sin was as black as could be,
Jesus came forth to be born of a virgin—
Dwelt amongst men, my example is He!

Living, He loved me; dying, He saved me;
Buried, He carried my sins far away;
Rising, He justified freely forever:
One day He's coming—oh, glorious day!

—Dr. J. Wilbur Chapman

I

THE SAVIOR IN LIFE AND DEATH

I. *The Savior's Sinless Life*

That our Lord lived a sinless life is the abundant testimony of Scripture. In this He was the most unique Person that ever lived or ever shall live. The Lord Himself said to those who were accusing Him of falsehood, "Which of you convinceth me of sin? And if I say the truth, why do ye not believe me?" (John 8:46).

Friends of Christ, those who were closest to Him, were not hesitant to ascribe sinlessness to Him. Listen to their testimonies: ". . . In him is no sin" (1 John 3:5); ". . . he . . . knew no sin . . ." (2 Cor. 5:21); "Who did no sin, neither was guile found in his mouth" (1 Pet. 2:22).

Enemies of Christ were no less hesitant to admit His absolute perfection. Judas' words of remorse and regret still echo down the corridors of time: "I have sinned in that I have betrayed the innocent blood" (Matt. 27:4). A similar testimony came from some who were responsible for His death: "Truly this was the Son of God" (Matt. 27:54). To admit that Jesus Christ was the Son of God is tantamount to admitting His sinlessness, for God is sinless. Even Pilate, who had made several futile attempts to get Jesus off his hands, had to admit ultimately to his hecklers that Jesus, as far as he was concerned, was a "just person" (Matt. 27:24) who did not deserve to die.

Not only did Christ succeed in living a sinless life, but He was incapable of sin. It was utterly impossible for Him to commit sin either in thought, word or deed since He did not possess the root cause of sin—the sin nature. New Testament writers present Him not only as one who triumphed over sin but also as one who could not sin. There is general agreement among those who accept the true deity of Christ that He was tempted and that He did not succumb to the temptation. There has been disagreement, though, over whether Christ simply did not sin or whether He could not have sinned. Both Scripture and reason insist upon what theologians call the impeccability of Christ. That is, Christ could not sin. If it be true that individual acts of sin are the result of the indwelling sin nature, most assuredly Christ could not have sinned because He did not possess a sin nature, which others receive from their parents through physical birth. The writer to the Hebrews put it this way: He was ". . . tempted like as we are, yet without sin" (Heb. 4:15). Of this latter phrase, "without sin," Robertson says, "There was no latent sin in Jesus to be stirred by temptation and no habits of sin to overcome."[1] Evidence for the absence of the root of sin in Christ, which produces the fruit, may also be found in the testimonies of John and Paul cited above (1 John 3:5; 2 Cor. 5:21). Furthermore, from a purely logical standpoint, if Christ could have sinned while here on earth, what would keep Him from sinning now? He is no more God now than He was then!

Some have assumed on the basis of the sinless nature and sinless life of Christ that therefore His life as well as His death provided substitution for man's sin. One writer puts it thus: "The Scriptures teach us plainly that Christ's *obedience* was as truly vicarious as was his *suffering,* and that he reconciled us to the Father by the one as well as by the other [italics

---

[1] A. T. Robertson, *Word Pictures in the New Testament* (Nashville: Broadman Press, 1932), V, p. 365.

mine]."[2] Usually His sufferings in life are said to constitute His active obedience, and His sufferings in death His passive obedience.[3] Now it cannot be denied that Christ suffered in life *and* death. But that His life sufferings were vicarious and substitutionary is open to serious question.

It is not difficult at all to imagine something of the grief and agony which must have been His as His holy person came into contact with wicked and ungodly sinners. We are sinners and yet we often suffer conflict and agony of soul as we hear men curse and deny the blessed Son of God. Was not Lot's righteous soul disturbed by the wicked deeds of the dwellers of Sodom (2 Pet. 2:7, 8)? How much more must He have been afflicted since He was infinitely pure and holy. Surely the righteous and holy nature of Christ was offended as He associated with corrupt and sinful humanity. He suffered in life because He was the sinless one in the midst of sinners, the righteous in the presence of the unrighteous. What agony of soul must have been His as He lived and moved among the ungodly and the Christ-rejectors of Adam's race!

Christ was the divine revealer of God and His will (John 1:18) and was thus frequently moved with compassion for the individual (Mark 1:41) and the multitudes (Matt. 9:36). This means He suffered in that He was a man of sorrows, bearing our griefs (Isa. 53:3, 4), and touched with the feeling of our infirmities (Heb. 4:15). The Gospel writers present Him as the compassionate Jesus whose compassion involved more than pity. He was moved to action by His understanding and sorrow for man's condition.

Centuries before Christ was born, Isaiah the prophet spoke of His life and death sufferings, clearly distinguishing between the two: "Surely he hath borne our griefs, and carried our sorrows: yet we did esteem him stricken, smitten of God, and afflicted. But he was wounded for our transgressions, he was bruised for our iniquities: the chastisement of our peace was upon him; and with his stripes we are healed. All we like sheep

---

[2] Archibald Alexander Hodge, *The Atonement* (Grand Rapids: Wm. B. Eerdmans Publishing Co., 1953), pp. 248, 249.
[3] *Ibid.*, pp. 248-264.

have gone astray; we have turned every one to his own way; and the LORD hath laid on him the iniquity of us all" (Isa. 53:4-6). According to Matthew, the Lord fulfilled the first part of verse 4 of Isaiah's prophecy during His life of earthly ministry before the cross as He cast out demons and healed all that were sick (Matt. 8:17).

The Apostle Peter records words similar to those of Isaiah in 53:5. Peter says Christ "bare our sins in his own body on the tree, that we, being dead to sins, should live unto righteousness: by whose stripes ye were healed" (1 Pet. 2:24). Even though Peter does not claim to be quoting Isaiah, there is surely an obvious similarity and relationship between 1 Peter 2:24 and Isaiah 53:5. In both instances the central idea is spiritual healing which is related to Christ's death and not the physical healing which He performed in His holy life.

Thus Isaiah's prophecy distinguishes between the life sufferings of Christ in which He sympathetically identified Himself with our physical infirmities and sicknesses (Isa. 53:4; Matt. 8:17) and the death sufferings through which Christ made provision for our spiritual sicknesses (Isa. 53:5, 6; 1 Pet. 2:24). Therefore, Christ's identification with man's physical griefs and sorrows was in His sinless life, and His identification with man's transgressions and iniquities was in His substitutionary death when He was stricken, smitten, afflicted and forsaken of God. The point of emphasis here, however, is that the Savior suffered during His earthly life and that suffering is associated with His divine compassion. Perhaps Christ's sufferings in life could be regarded as a divine preview or the firstfruits of what was to take place on the cross.

The anticipation of the cross was ever before Christ, and this brought suffering to Him since He knew the awful price which He was to pay for sin. The revelation and understanding of what it meant to bear in His body the sins of the world and to become an offering for sin did not suddenly dawn upon Christ while on the cross. He knew the purpose for which He had come into the world, and the cross was ever before Him. Nowhere is this more clearly revealed than in His Gethsemane experience (Matt. 26:37-42). Here we are given insight into something which the Savior often faced in anticipation of Golgotha, and we are also informed of His attitude of absolute surrender to the will of His Father.

Real though the life sufferings of Christ surely were, yet they are viewed in Scripture as non-atoning. Only as the Savior becomes a curse hanging on the accursed tree do you have substitution for sin. By divine design it was not the blood shed at the time of His circumcision or in the Garden of Gethsemane, but rather His blood shed on the cross which made an atonement for sin. He ". . . made peace through the blood of his cross . . ." (Col. 1:20). It was not the amount of suffering which made the acceptable substitution for sin but the nature of that suffering. Scripture simply does not support the idea that Christ's life of sufferings and life of perfect obedience to the law provided a substitution for sin and earned for His own the reward of eternal life. He was made sin for us on the cross, not in His life. Thus Peter could say, "Who his own self bare our sins in his own body on the tree . . ." (1 Pet. 2:24).

It must be granted that He "learned" obedience in the things which He suffered (Heb. 5:8). But nowhere is it declared that this obedience in life was substitutionary or vicarious in nature. In fact, His life of obedience is frequently associated with His work on the cross. For example, He is said to have come to do the will of God, which will of God culminated in "the offering of the body of Jesus Christ once for all" (Heb. 10:7-10). Or, again, note Paul's declaration of His obedience unto death, "even the death of the cross" (Phil. 2:8), which evidently was a particular kind of obedience. Surely we are not to understand by this emphasis upon Christ's obedience and learning of it that He learned to obey as men learn to obey. He need not learn that because He never disobeyed the Father. As a man, however, He did learn what obedience costs.

Christ's one righteous act of obedience which provided justification was His death on the cross (Rom. 5:18). This one act of obedience by Christ is contrasted with the one act of disobedience by Adam which brought all men to condemnation. "For as by one man's disobedience many were made sinners, so by the obedience of one shall many be made righteous" (Rom.

5:19). Nowhere in Scripture is the life of Christ ever viewed as that which accounts men as righteous. Speaking of the "obedience of the one" in the above passage, Vine said: "Here again the reference is not to the life of Christ but to the culminating act of His obedience in His Death on the Cross, the same act as is described in verse 18 as 'one act of righteousness.' That is the means of justification (see 5:9). The description, 'act of righteousness,' presents the legal aspect of the Death of Christ."[4]

In summary, it could be said that all of Christ's life sufferings, though non-atoning in themselves, did prepare Him, qualify Him and prove Him to be a qualified sacrifice for sin. So that He might be qualified to offer Himself as a sacrifice for sin to God, it was imperative that He be sinless, perfect God. Likewise, that He may be man's substitute, He had to be a perfect man. Without a sinless life He could not have offered a sinless sacrifice. Yet the Bible attributes substitution for sin only to His death.

II. *The Savior's Substitutionary Death*

Many were the accomplishments of the Savior in His death. Through His death, Christ ended the Mosaic law as a rule of life (Heb. 7:11; 2 Cor. 3:6-11).[5] "For the law was given by Moses, but grace and truth came by Jesus Christ" (John 1:17). The benefits of His death were directed toward sin in providing redemption (paying the purchase price, Gal. 3:13), toward man in providing reconciliation (changing the relation of the world to Himself, 2 Cor. 5:17-19) and toward God in providing propitiation (a satisfaction, 1 John 2:2). Every provision for living the spiritual life finds its source in the work of Christ on the cross. However, and without doubt, the most important accomplishment of Christ's death, and the one on which all the others depend, was His substitution for sin and sinners. He did not

⁴ W. E. Vine, *The Epistle to the Romans* (London: Oliphants Limited, 1948), pp. 83, 84.
⁵ For an excellent discussion of the ending of the law of Moses as a rule of life and the continuance of the moral law of God, see Roy L. Aldrich, *Holding Fast to Grace* (Findlay, Ohio: Dunham Publishing Co., n.d.).

die merely to demonstrate bravery in the hour of death. He did not die simply for the benefit of men. Nor did he die as a victim of His persecutors. Rather, He died in the place of sinners. His death was vicarious in that He was the sinless vicar intervening for man. The Savior took the sinner's place and thus acted as the sinner's substitute. The certainty and finality of this substitution is true whether anyone ever appropriates it by faith or not. In other words, its reality and value do not depend upon its application to the individual.

The Scriptures use two Greek words which denote substitution. The Savior used the stronger of these two words as He spoke to the disciples concerning His purpose in giving His life. When tempted to exalt themselves, they were to remember that the one desiring to be greatest among them was to be their servant, "Even as the Son of man came not to be ministered unto, but to minister, and to give his life a ransom for many" (Matt. 20:28; Mark 10:45). Here the Greek preposition *anti* is translated "for." This word clearly denotes substitution, "in the place of" or "instead of" another. It was so used in the Septuagint or Greek translation of the Old Testament. For example, ". . . For God, said she, hath appointed me another seed *instead of* Abel, whom Cain slew" (Gen. 4:25). Or, ". . . Joseph gave them bread *in exchange for* horses, and . . . flocks, and . . . cattle" (Gen. 47:17). There are numerous other passages, which are unrelated to Christ's work on the cross, where this idea of substitution is the only possible meaning.

In the New Testament this preposition is employed in the same sense: ". . . Archelaus did reign in Judea *in the room of* his father Herod . . ." (Matt. 2:22); "Ye have heard that it hath been said, An eye *for* an eye, and a tooth *for* a tooth" (Matt. 5:38); "Recompense to no man evil *for* evil" (Rom. 12:17). It should be noted that in the instances cited above as well as in many others, *anti*, "for," is used in passages totally unrelated to redemption, and it has the same meaning of substitution. "Nor is it less so, assuredly, in our Lord's statement, 'The Son of man is come to give His life a ransom for many. . . .' Indeed, were there any room for doubt as to the proper import of the preposition in the present instance, the doubt would be at once removed by its connection with the word *lutron* which indicates that the life of the Son of Man was 'the ransom given for many,' or the price paid to redeem their forfeited lives."[6]

The other Greek word sometimes used to denote substitution is *huper*. The basic meaning is "for the benefit of" or "in behalf of"; but it also means in some contexts what *anti* means—"substitution," "in the place of," or "in the stead of." In John 13:37, when Peter said to the Lord, "I will lay down my life for thy sake," he used *huper* and obviously meant "in behalf of" or "for the benefit of." Again, when the Savior said, "Pray *for* them which despitefully use you" (Matt. 5:44), He meant, "Pray on behalf of them or for their benefit."

That *huper* also denotes the idea of substitution is proved not only from its use in the Greek classics but also from the New Testament itself. Paul used the word in his Epistle to Philemon regarding Onesimus: "Whom I would have retained with me, that *in thy stead (huper)* he might have ministered unto me . . ." (Philemon 13). The apostle was not asking for the slave to minister "for the benefit of" Philemon, but "in the place of" himself. The point to be made here is this: if *huper* has the meaning of substitution in a context totally unrelated to salvation, then it can also have that meaning when it is used in relation to the redemptive work of Christ. Therefore, we conclude that while *anti* only connotes substitution, *huper* connotes both the idea of benefit "in behalf of" another and also the idea of substitution. This latter meaning is clearly meant in such statements as Christ ". . . gave himself a ransom for all . . ." (1 Tim. 2:6); Christ tasted ". . . death for every man . . ." (Heb. 2:9); Christ ". . . suffered . . . the just for the unjust . . ." (1 Pet. 3:18); and "For he hath made him to be sin for us, who knew no sin; that we might be made the righteousness of God in him" (2 Cor. 5:21).

III. *Theories of the Savior's Death*

A look at the history of the doctrine of the atonement with

---

[6]Thomas Crawford, *The Doctrine of the Atonement* (Grand Rapids: Baker Book House, 1954), p. 21.

the many theories[7] which men have devised will quickly reveal
the seriousness and the extent of the departure from the Biblical
message of the substitutionary nature of Christ's sacrifice.

The early church was plagued with the false notion that
Christ's death was a ransom paid to Satan so that Satan's claims
on man could be released. Others in the early church, such as
Irenaeus, believed Christ recapitulated in Himself or went
through all the stages of human life, including those which involve sin.

In the eleventh century the satisfaction or commercial
theory was advanced by Anselm. He believed the honor of God
was robbed by the sin of man, and thus Christ died to vindicate
God's honor. God, in this view, could have done this either
by punishment or satisfaction, and He chose the latter through
the gift of His Son. While this theory has much to merit it,
its weakness lies in the fact that it grounds the necessity of the
atonement in God's honor rather than in His justice.

The theory of Abelard arose in opposition to Anselm's theory. Abelard's moral influence theory finds many advocates today. "The fundamental idea is that there is no principle of
the divine nature which necessarily calls for satisfaction on the
part of the sinner; and that the death of Christ should not be
regarded as an expiation for sin. It was merely a manifesta-
tion of the love of God, suffering in and with His sinful creatures, and taking upon Himself their woes and griefs."[8]

About the sixteenth century the Socinians postulated the
idea that Christ died as an example. This they did in opposition
to the view of the reformers that Christ vicariously atoned for
sinners. In this example theory, Christ did not atone for sin
in any sense, and salvation comes to man by Christ's example
of faith and obedience.

As a compromise view between that of the reformers and
the Socinian idea, a view called the governmental theory was
adopted. Adherents of this view advocated that God altered
His demands, and although sinners deserved death because of

[7] For an excellent survey see L. Berkhof, *Systematic Theology* (Grand
Rapids: Wm. B. Eerdmans Publishing Co., 1953), pp. 348ff.
[8] *Ibid.*, p. 386.

sin, He allowed Christ to render a kind of satisfaction which He accepted to show His displeasure with sin but which was not the kind of satisfaction He could have demanded.

Other views and variations of views prevailed, all of which attempted to explain the person and work of Christ without accepting His sinless life and substitutionary death. The mystical theory was, and still is, one such view. There is a great deal of similarity between the moral influence theory and the mystical theory; in fact, some view it as a modern variation of the moral influence idea. In this mystical view the purpose of the incarnation was to lift man to the plane of the divine. The view insists that while Christ possessed a human nature that was corrupt, the Holy Spirit kept Him from manifesting the corruption and thus purified human nature so that in His death He could remove original depravity.

Perhaps the most subtle theory in the history of the church was proposed by McLeod Campbell. His view of vicarious repentance, as the title indicates, includes the idea of substitution. However, the substitutionary element relates to Christ's death as a confession or repentance for man's guilt, and not to Christ's death as the actual payment for sin. Thus, only the repentance is substitutionary, not the death itself.

The greatest difficulty with most of these views lies in the fact that they emphasize only one aspect of truth and either neglect or deny other truths. Most of the above-mentioned views contain elements of truth, but they all fail to ascribe to Christ's death what He and the writers of the New Testament ascribed to it, namely, vicarious substitution. While it is true that Christ was a perfect example and that He satisfied God's honor and government, the purpose of His death goes far beyond these according to Scripture, where we are told that He died in the stead of and in the place of sinners. Perhaps the reason for such weak and incomplete views stems from weak views of sin and man's total inability. If man is not seen as a rebel against God and sin is not seen as an infinitely heinous crime against God, the necessity of the vicarious atonement of Christ will, of course, be nullified. And many today, like the men who introduced these theories of the atonement into the church, reject the Biblical concept of man as destitute of righteousness and hence reject also the need for a substitutionary atonement.

One such non-evangelical spokesman for contemporary theology put it this way: "That man sins no one will deny. . . . But that a curse is upon man because of the sin of the first man is to me an immoral absurdity."[9] With such a rejection of man's absolute sinfulness, this same writer could say of Christ's atonement: "I have never been able to carry the idea of justice to the place where someone else can vicariously pay for what I have done in order to clean the slate. . . . It simply does not make sense to me. It is rather an offense. It offends my moral sense."[10]

Another, with equal fervor and dogmatism, rejects the idea of substitution by Christ by saying, "Certainly we ought to repudiate the notion that God is unwilling to forgive any sin until blood has been spilled as propitiation."[11] Strange it is that today with all the talk about "rediscovering the Bible," reading it from "within," returning to the "theology of Jesus," and "Biblical theology," there is so little acceptance of what the Bible actually has to say on the matters in question.

IV. *The Two Sides of the Cross*

Who was responsible for the death of Christ? This question has puzzled the minds of men ever since Christ was put to death, and it has been revived recently in the fourth session of Vatican Two. There has always been an attempt to shift the guilt of that dastardly deed from one group to another. Scripture assigns responsibility to three realms—the divine, the angelic and the human.

In both the Old and New Testaments the divine responsibility is clearly taught. Isaiah the prophet said, ". . . The Lord hath laid on him the iniquity of us all" (Isa. 53:6). Paul the apostle said, "For he [God] hath made him to be sin for us . . ." (2 Cor. 5:21). Jesus Christ Himself said of His life, "No man taketh

---

[9] G. Bromley Oxnam, *A Testament of Faith* (Boston: Little, Brown and Company, 1958), p. 40.

[10] *Ibid.*, pp. 39, 41.

[11] L. Harold DeWolf, *The Case for Theology in Liberal Perspective* (Philadelphia: The Westminster Press, 1959), p. 77.

it from me, but I lay it down of myself. I have power to lay it down, and I have power to take it again. This commandment have I received of my Father" (John 10:18). The acceptance of divine responsibility does not mean, of course, that the Godhead accepts the responsibility for the human sin involved in the crucifixion of Christ. God never accepts the responsibility for sin even when that sin is committed in the course of the fulfillment of prophecy. This acknowledgment of divine involvement does mean though that from eternity past God had devised a plan whereby His Son would provide redemption for Adam's fallen race (Acts 2:23; 4:27, 28; 1 Pet. 1:20).

Within the divine sovereign plan Satan must also be held responsible for Christ's death. This is forcefully disclosed in the protevangelium of Genesis 3:15 where it is disclosed that Satan is to bruise the heel of the seed of the woman. The wound which the serpent was to inflict, and did inflict at the time of the crucifixion, was not a mortal wound; yet it was a diabolic attempt to do directly or through men everything possible to destroy the Savior. The Savior's wound to Satan was prophesied to be mortal since He was to "bruise his head," and this was the exact nature of the wound and outcome of the struggle between Satan and Christ. Christ said in prospect of His work on the cross, "Now is the judgment of this world: now shall the prince of this world be cast out" (John 12:31). Added proof of Christ's victory over Satan, in spite of his subtle attempts, is the resurrection, which becomes a divine guarantee for the defeat and ultimate doom of the Devil and also for the future resurrection of the child of God.

Mankind in no way escapes responsibility for the death of Christ because that death was a part of a divine plan nor because Scripture assigns responsibility to Satan. Inexplainable as the association may be to man's mind, Scripture unites what the divine counsel determined should take place at Calvary with the actions of human beings. "For of a truth against thy holy child Jesus, whom thou hast anointed, both Herod, and Pontius Pilate, with the Gentiles, and the people of Israel, were gathered together, For to do whatsoever thy hand and thy counsel determined before to be done" (Acts 4:27, 28). Here in one sweeping statement Herod the king, Pilate the governor, along with all the Gentiles and the people of Israel, are said to be responsible for Christ's death, which death was determined by divine counsel in eternity past. Added to this is the abundant testimony of Scripture that Christ died for "sinners," "the ungodly," "the unjust," and that He provided redemption, reconciliation and propitiation for all men, thus indicating that the whole human race is responsible for His death. It was the sin of the race that made necessary the Savior's death, since in their lost condition no distinction is ever made in Scripture between elect sinners and nonelect ones.

The cross of Christ, therefore, demonstrates and reveals two extremes. It declares the immensity of God's love in giving His Son and the enormity of man's guilt in crucifying the Lord of glory. Calvary has two sides—the side of gloom and the side of glory. There is man's side; there is God's side.

The side of gloom is unveiled when we learn that the sinless Christ died at the hands of sinful men. One must ask with the hymn writer, "Was ever crime so wrong?" The answer is no! No greater crime has ever been committed or recorded in all the annals of history—sacred or secular. Not only are crime and gloom seen in that wicked and sinful men put the sinless and perfect Lamb of God to death; they are also revealed by the reaction of heaven and earth to the brutal business done at Calvary. The heavens displayed shame by becoming dark for three hours. The earth quaked and trembled in anger, as it were. It seems as though the earth was threatening to swallow the creatures who had put the Creator to death (Matt. 27:45-51). Yes, from every conceivable human vantage point, the crucifixion was a crime of stupendous proportion, and, from the perspective of the unregenerate, that is all it was—a human tragedy.

But the cross was not an accident which defeated the purpose of God or which caught Him off guard. It is true that Christ was crucified by wicked hands, but it is also true that He was "delivered by the determinate counsel and foreknowledge of God . . ." (Acts 2:23) and "slain from the foundation of the world" (Rev. 13:8). If the crime and gloom of Golgotha are evidenced by the sin committed there, the glory is seen in the divine accomplishments and exaltation of the Savior. For the Father took Christ, the rejected one, and brought triumph to Himself through the very event men view as a tragedy. He took the gloom and sorrow and turned it into glory, grace and salvation. The very One Whom sinful men spit upon and debased, that One the sovereign God raised from the dead, exalted to His own right hand and gave a name above every other name (Phil. 2:9-11).

Not only is mankind responsible for the death of Christ but, according to Scripture, the very necessity of the atonement arises from man's sin. Why did the Father smite His Son, turn His back on Him and put to grief the very One He loved and in whom He was well pleased? The answer to this baffling question was given by the Apostle Paul. Speaking of Christ, he said: "Whom God hath set forth to be a propitiation through faith in his blood, to declare his righteousness for the remission of sins that are past, through the forbearance of God; To declare, I say, at this time his righteousness: that he might be just, and the justifier of him which believeth in Jesus" (Rom. 3:25, 26).

Here Paul not only declared the nature of the atonement—Christ being "set forth to be a propitiation through faith in his blood"—but also the necessity of the atonement—"to declare . . . his righteousness: that he might be just, and the justifier of him which believeth in Jesus." That is, the Father would not have been just nor could He have been the Justifier apart from Christ's death in the place of sinners. Therefore it was man's sin, sin for which man alone is responsible, that made necessary the death of Christ.

Grace! 'tis a charming sound,
Harmonious to the ear;
Heav'n with the echo shall resound,
And all the earth shall hear.

Saved by grace alone!
This is all my plea:
Jesus died for all mankind,
And Jesus died for me.

—P. Doddridge

II

THE DIVINE PURPOSE OF THE ATONEMENT

I. *The Real Issue*

The task before us in this chapter is to discover a Biblical answer to the question, "Why did Christ die?" After settling that issue, we will then be in a position to ask a second question, "What is the extent of the atonement?" or "For whom did Christ die?" Admittedly, there are problems on both sides of the question. One who desires to be true to the revelation of Scripture must be careful not to become a slave of any man-made system of theology. The question is not, "What did the reformers believe and teach?" or "Shall I be a Calvinist or an Arminian?" nor even, "What is the historical view of the church?" as important and helpful as these matters are; but the crux of the matter is, "What saith the Scriptures?"

There is no question about it; the issue between limited and unlimited atonement centers in the design or purpose of the redemptive work of Christ. Evangelicals on both sides agree that not all will be saved. Therefore, the extent of the atonement or the answer to the question, "For whom did Christ die?" can be given only by understanding the divine intent of the Father in the death of His Son. Loraine Boettner put it succinctly when he said, "The nature of the atonement settles its extent."[1] This clear-cut issue is not always understood. Too often the determining of limited or unlimited atonement is pictured as a choice between Calvinism and Arminianism. It should be clearly understood that one need not be an Arminian simply because he rejects limited atonement. On the other hand, one is certainly not a Calvinist just because he accepts limited atonement. In other words, there are other and more serious differences between Calvinistic and Arminian theology, and even between these two systems and other systems, than simply the extent of the atonement.

The fact of the matter is that a good many today who are proud to embrace Calvinism fail to realize that Calvinism involves far more than the acceptance of the five famous points. This is especially true of premillennialists and dispensationalists who claim to be Calvinists. Christians of these persuasions must be aware of the fact that Calvinism is a system of theology which has come to embrace covenant theology and amillennialism and is, therefore, in direct opposition to both premillennialism and dispensationalism.

The same could be said for Arminianism. To say one is an Arminian means not only that he rejects the five points of Calvinism, but also that he accepts a *system* of theology, for that is what Arminianism is.

It seems far better to say that one believes this .tenet or that one as he may find agreement with it in the Bible than to imply acceptance of an entire system unless the individual is prepared to accept the whole theological structure. The desire and goal of the child of God must not be adherence to a humanly-constructed system simply for the sake of tradition or church relations. Let us be Biblicists above everything else and at all costs; and when and where this position conflicts with man-made systems of theology, let it be!

There is an increasing number of individuals who wholeheartedly accept four of the famous five points of Calvinism,

[1] Loraine Boettner, *The Reformed Doctrine of Predestination* (Philadelphia: The Presbyterian and Reformed Publishing Co., 1965), p. 152.

although they reject limited atonement, or as it is sometimes called, particular redemption. These should probably be referred to as moderate Calvinists because, while they believe in total depravity, unconditional election, irresistible grace and the perseverance of the saints, they do not hold to limited atonement.

Their refusal to believe that Christ died only for the elect does not make them Arminians any more than it makes them universalists. They differ drastically with both the Arminians and the universalists. These moderate Calvinists differ with the Arminians because they do not believe all men are born with sufficient grace or divine favor to believe in Christ but rather that all men are born totally dead in trespasses and sins, possessing no divine favor and incapable of doing anything to merit the favor of God. They differ with the universalists because they do not believe Christ's death for all means all will eventually and ultimately be saved. Instead, they believe only those who appropriate the death of Christ by personal faith because they have been chosen by a sovereign God will be saved.

Since, as was indicated earlier, the real question centers in the design or purpose of the atonement, and since there are two opposing schools of thought within orthodoxy, it would be well to find the answer set forth by Arminians, Calvinists and then from the Scriptures. All other questions and answers are secondary to the settling of the extent of the atonement. Why did God the Son die on the accursed tree? That is the question. When it is answered we will have discovered the extent of the atonement and the people for whom Christ died.

II. *The Arminian Answer*

James Arminius (1560-1609) was a noted professor of theology at the University of Leyden in Leyden, Holland. After his appointment to answer the attacks being made upon supralapsarianism, or hyper-Calvinism,[2] which led him to accept a less

---

[2] The "lapsarian" controversy concerns the logical order of the decrees of God. Actually, there is only one decree or plan of God with many parts. Scripture simply does not state the order in which God planned the various stages of His plan. In fact, it is even questionable whether God ever viewed them as separate items anyway. It would be more in keeping with the char-

severe type of Calvinism, he became the central figure in the theological controversy of his day in the Dutch Reformed Church. As is usually the case, the followers of Arminius have distorted his views. What passes today as Arminianism would hardly be identifiable with that which Arminius set forth in his Declaration of Sentiments delivered to the states of Holland in October of 1608.[3]

Just one year after the death of Arminius a group of his followers drew up five articles of faith in the form of a protest commonly called the Remonstrance or the Five Arminian Articles. These articles were in opposition to those parts of the Belgic Confession of Faith and the Heidelberg Catechism which stressed what came to be known as the five points of Calvinism, which were later set forth at the Synod of Dort (1618-1619).

Though our purpose here is not to deal with each of the "five points" of Arminianism but only the one pertaining to the atonement, it will be well to summarize the five. Roger Nicole has done this very accurately for us: "I. God elects or reproves on the basis of foreseen faith or unbelief. II. Christ died for all men and for every man, although only believers are saved. III. Man is so depraved that divine grace is necessary unto faith or any good deed. IV. This grace may be resisted. V. Whether

---

acter of God to say that He conceived of each part and the whole of His sovereign decree at one time. At any rate, theologians have attempted to arrange a logical order for the various parts of God's plan. The word "lapsarian" comes from the Latin *lapsus* meaning "fall." When the prefix *supra*, meaning "above," appears, it means placing the decree of God to elect men before His decree to allow the fall of man. At the time of Arminius supralapsarianism was being circulated by Dirck Coornhert (1522-1590). This extreme view has been modified by many who call themselves Calvinists today. Many Calvinists adopt the infralapsarian view instead. This view places the decree to elect some from among the sinful race after the decree to permit the fall. Still others prefer the sublapsarian view which places the decree to elect not only after the fall but also after the decree to provide salvation for all. Calvinists are found among all three of these positions and these are all in opposition to the Arminian view which, though it is identical to the sublapsarian view, makes salvation depend on foreseen human virtue and faith. Though John Calvin does not directly discuss this particular issue, most of his followers believe he held to infralapsarianism and can find nothing to the contrary in his writings.

[3] See *The Works of James Arminius, D.D.,* Vol. I, trans. James Nichols (Buffalo: Derby, Miller and Orton, 1853).

all who are truly regenerate will certainly persevere in the faith is a point which needs further investigation."[4]

It will be well now to see the full statement regarding the atonement set forth in the Remonstrance. This will help us understand the answer of Arminianism to the question of the divine design of the atonement. Article II of the Remonstrance reads as follows: "That . . . Jesus Christ, the Saviour of the world, died for all men and for every man, so that he has *obtained for them all, by his death on the cross, redemption and the forgiveness of sins* [italics mine]; yet that no one actually enjoys this forgiveness of sins except the believer, according to the word of the Gospel of John 3:16, 'God so loved the world that he gave his only-begotten Son, that whosoever believeth in him should not perish, but have everlasting life.' And in the First Epistle of John 2:2: 'And he is the propitiation for our sins; and not for ours only, but also for the sins of the whole world.' "[5]

The crucial point of this statement regarding the purpose and extent of the atonement centers in the word "obtained." This is precisely the Arminian view, not only that Christ's death *provided* salvation for all but that His death *obtained* it for all. This explains, of course, why Arminianism believes each member of Adam's race possesses sufficient grace to be saved. In the Arminian concept, God has endowed every man with a grace or favor which enables him to repent and believe, if he will. From the Confession of the Arminian Remonstrance comes this statement which clarifies the above observation: "Although there is the greatest diversity in the degrees in which grace is bestowed in accordance with the Divine will, yet the Holy Spirit confers, or at least is ready to confer, upon all and each to whom the Word is ordinarily preached, as much grace as is sufficient for generating faith and carrying forward their conversion in its successive stages. This sufficient grace for faith and conversion is allotted not only to those who actually believe and are converted, but

---

[4] Roger Nicole, "Arminianism," *Baker's Dictionary of Theology,* ed. Everett F. Harrison (Grand Rapids: Baker Book House, 1960), p. 64.

[5] Philip Schaff, *The Creeds of Christendom,* III (New York: Harper and Son Publishers, 1919).

also to those who do not actually believe, and are not in fact
converted" (Confession, chapter XVII).[6]

In the Arminian concept this means of course that on the
basis of Christ's death, and because He *obtained* forgiveness of
sins for all, every man now has a degree of grace sufficient to
generate faith and repentance if the man yields to it. Viewing
it from another perspective, this means the one who does not
believe does not because he lacks some human efficiency or ability
to cooperate with God. This places man in the position then in
which he determines whether the sufficient grace he possesses
will or will not become effectual. To say the least, this view removes God too much from the great work of salvation. Instead
of salvation being a work of God, it becomes a work of God
and man. It places God on the periphery as a bystander, having
given all men a measure of grace which may or may not become
effectual, depending solely upon how they respond to it.

Without going into a lengthy discussion of this view, it must
be said that this strikes at the very heart of that great Biblical
doctrine of total depravity. Total depravity means that man possesses nothing nor can he do anything to merit favor before
God. Scripture is abundantly clear on this point. According to
the Word of God, this condition affects not only every man but
also every part of every man (Rom. 1—3). All unsaved men are
viewed by God as "lost" (Luke 19:10), "condemned" (John 3:18),
under the "wrath of God" (John 3:36), "dead in trespasses and
sins" (Eph. 2:1, 2) and as possessing a heart that is "desperately
wicked" (Jer. 17:9).

Strange as it may seem, in light of their view of sufficient
grace, Arminians nevertheless speak frequently of man's lost condition. Watson, an outstanding Arminian theologian, cites abundant testimony from history and then from Scripture for the
corrupt and degenerate condition of all men.[7]

Watson proceeds to summarize his view and that of Arminians in general, and in the process he destroys the clear teach-

---

[6] Cited by William G. T. Shedd, *Calvinism: Pure and Mixed* (New York:
Charles Scribner's Sons, 1893), p. 102.
[7] Richard Watson, *Theological Institutes* (New York: Carlton & Porter,
n.d.), II, pp. 61-80.

ing of Scripture and thus reveals the weakness of the Arminian position. "From this view of the total alienation of the nature of man from God, it does not, however, follow that there should be nothing virtuous and praiseworthy among men, until, in the proper sense, they become the subjects of the regeneration insisted upon in the Gospel as necessary to qualify men for the kingdom of heaven. From the virtues which have existed among heathens, and from men being called upon to repent and believe the Gospel, it has been argued that human nature is not so entirely corrupt and disabled as the above representation would suppose; and, indeed, on the Calvinistic theory, which denies that all men are interested in the benefits procured by the death of Christ, it would be extremely difficult for any to meet this objection, and to maintain their own views of the corruption of man with consistency. On the contrary theory of God's universal love nothing is more easy; because, in consequence of the atonement offered for all, the Holy Spirit is administered to all, and to his secret operations all that is really spiritual and good, in its principle, is to be ascribed."[8]

It would seem then that while the Arminian acknowledges the scriptural teaching of man's lost condition, he softens that teaching by his doctrine of sufficient grace. Since this point is so crucial to our discussion, it seems necessary again to quote Watson in demonstration of how man's lost condition is countered by sufficient grace procured at Calvary for all.

"It is allowed, and all Scriptural advocates of the universal redemption of mankind will join with the Calvinists in maintaining the doctrine, that every disposition and inclination to good which originally existed in the nature of man is lost by the fall; that all men, in their simply *natural* state, are 'dead in trespasses and sins,' and have neither the will nor the power to turn to God; and that no one is sufficient of himself to think or do any thing of a saving tendency. But, as all men are required to do those things which have a saving tendency, we contend that the grace to do them has been bestowed upon all."[9]

---

[8] *Ibid.*, p. 83.
[9] *Ibid.*, p. 447.

In reality, then, Arminianism rejects the truth that every man is born totally incapable of doing anything to merit favor with God or even to move toward God, and, rather, gives to man a measure of grace which makes him acceptable to God if only man will add his part and accept God. "According to the Arminian theory the atonement has simply made it possible for all men to cooperate with divine grace and thus save themselves—if they will."[10]

In conclusion, the point to be made here is that these other ideas regarding man's natural condition and native ability to cooperate with God stem from the idea that Christ's death *obtained* salvation for all and made possible sufficient grace for all to cooperate with God in salvation. This means in reality that the decision to believe or not to believe is quite unrelated to the electing purposes of God or the effectual working of the Holy Spirit but rests ultimately and entirely with the individual.

III. *The Strict Calvinistic Answer*

The views of the Arminians set forth in the Remonstrance of 1610 were examined and rejected as heretical at a national Synod in Dort, meeting from 1618 to November 13, 1619. Not only did the Synod reject the Remonstrance position but it also set out to present the true Calvinistic teaching in regard to the five matters called into question. This they accomplished by stating what we know today as the "five points of Calvinism." The term *Calvinism* was derived from the great reformer John Calvin (1509-1564), who along with many others expounded these views.

The "five points of Calvinism" presented at the Synod are as follows: (1) total depravity; (2) unconditional election; (3) limited atonement, or particular redemption; (4) irresistible grace, or the efficacious call of the Spirit; and (5) perseverance of the saints, or eternal security.

Concerning the third point, that of limited atonement, the Synod of Dort declared: "For this was the Sovereign counsel and most gracious will and purpose of God the Father, that the

---

[10] Boettner, *loc. cit.*

quickening and saving efficacy of the most precious death of his Son should extend to all the elect, for bestowing upon them alone the gift of justifying faith, thereby to bring them infallibly to salvation. . . ."[11]

From the day these words were uttered to the present day, many followers of Calvinism have understood this statement to teach limited or particular atonement. The design of the atonement according to Calvinists was to secure the salvation of the elect. The Calvinistic doctrine differs from the Arminian teaching in that Calvinists confine the atonement to the elect and view all men in their natural state as totally depraved, thus lacking any ability to cooperate with God in anything. That the design of the atonement was to save those for whom Christ died is not difficult to prove from the writings of Calvinists. Steele and Thomas state it bluntly: "Christ's redeeming work was intended to save the elect only and actually secured salvation for them. . . . The gift of faith is infallibly applied by the Spirit to all for whom Christ died, thereby guaranteeing their salvation."[12]

John Owen, the Calvinist of Calvinists, put it this way: ". . . Jesus Christ, according to the counsel and will of his Father, did offer himself upon the cross, to the procurement of those things before recounted, and maketh continual intercession, with this intent and purpose; *that all the good things so procured by his death, might be actually and infallibly bestowed on, and applied to, all and every one for whom he died* [italics mine], according to the will and purpose of God."[13]

John Murray asks and answers the questions at issue in typical Calvinistic fashion: "Did Christ come to make the salvation of all men possible, to remove obstacles that stood in the way of salvation, and merely to make provision for salvation? . . . Did he come to put all men in a savable state? Or did he come to secure the salvation of all those who are ordained to eternal

---

[11] Schaff, *op. cit.*

[12] David N. Steele and Curtis C. Thomas, *The Five Points of Calvinism Defined, Defended, Documented* (Philadelphia: The Presbyterian and Reformed Publishing Co., 1963), p. 17.

[13] John Owen, *The Works of John Owen,* ed. Thomas Cloutt (London: J. F. Dove, 1823), V, pp. 290, 291.

life? Did he come to make men redeemable? Or did he come effectually and infallibly to redeem? The doctrine of the atonement must be radically revised if, as atonement, it applies to those who finally perish as well as to those who are the heirs of eternal life. . . . This we cannot do. . . . If some of those for whom atonement was made and redemption wrought perish eternally, then the atonement is not itself efficacious. . . . We shall have none of it. The doctrine of 'limited atonement' which we maintain is the doctrine which limits the atonement to those who are heirs of eternal life, to the elect. That limitation insures its efficacy and conserves its essential character as efficient and effective redemption."[14]

Again, the same writer in another work said of the atonement: "If it accomplished all that is implied in the categories by which it is defined and if it secures and insures the consummating redemption, the design must be coextensive with the ultimate *result* [italics mine]."[15]

The theologian Charles Hodge voices the same view when he says, ". . . The righteousness of Christ did not make the salvation of men merely possible, it secured the actual salvation of those for whom He wrought."[16]

Speaking as a Calvinist and for Calvinism as opposed to Arminianism, R. B. Kuiper said: "Calvinism, on the contrary, insists that the atonement saves all whom it was intended to save."[17]

Thus, it should be clear that the answer of Calvinists as to the divine design and intent of the atonement was not merely to provide salvation but actually to secure it for the elect with no provision whatsoever for the nonelect. They view the work of Christ on the cross as efficacious in itself. In their view, the cross secures and applies its own benefits. The atoning work of Christ on the cross saves.

It must be remembered that the extent of the atonement or

[14] John Murray, *Redemption—Accomplished and Applied* (Grand Rapids: Wm. B. Eerdmans Publishing Co., 1955), pp. 73, 74.

[15] John Murray, *The Atonement* (Philadelphia: The Presbyterian and Reformed Publishing Co., 1962), p. 27.

[16] Cited by Boettner, *op. cit.,* p. 155.

[17] R. B. Kuiper, *For Whom Did Christ Die?* (Grand Rapids: Wm. B. Eerdmans Publishing Co., 1959), p. 73.

the answer to the question, "For whom did Christ die?" is determined by the design of the atonement. Some Calvinists limit the extent of the atonement to the elect simply because they believe it was designed in itself, and quite apart from anything else, to save. On the other hand, others who consider themselves moderate Calvinists reject limited atonement because they believe the design of the atonement provided a basis of salvation for those who believe (the elect), and a basis of condemnation for those who refuse to believe (the nonelect).

Though those among Calvinists who accept limited atonement thus confine the extent of the atonement to the elect, it should not be thought that they limit the sufficiency or value of Christ's death. This they do not do. The usual statement coming from them is to the effect that the death of Christ was *sufficient* for all men but *efficient* only for the elect. This statement is intended by limited redemptionists to satisfy those who object to their limited view. But does it really answer the difficulties raised by the scriptural passages which teach the universality of the atonement? What they really mean when they say Christ's death was *sufficient* for all is that His blood was of such infinite value that no more could have been required of the Father had He intended the Son's death to extend to all men.

Boettner attempts to correct the occasional misunderstanding of the Calvinist position by emphasizing that Christ did not suffer so much for one soul and so much for another, and by insisting that He would have suffered no more if more were to have been saved. Positively, he states, "We believe, however, that even if many or fewer of the human race were to have been pardoned and saved, an atonement of infinite value would have been necessary in order to have secured for them these blessings; and though many more, or even all men were to have been pardoned and saved, the sacrifice of Christ would have been amply sufficient as the ground or basis of their salvation."[18]

Or again, as another Calvinist has put it, "Thus Christ's saving work was limited in that it was designed to save some and

---

[18] Boettner, *op. cit.*, pp. 151, 152.

not others, but it was not limited in value for it was of infinite worth and would have secured salvation for everyone if that had been God's intention."[19]

Now this all sounds fine, but it does not mean, as some suppose, that God actually intended Christ's death to be all-encompassing in its scope. When this *sufficiency* of the death of Christ for all is admitted by the limited redemptionists, they are still insisting that Christ died only for the elect and merely admitting that had it been the desire of God He could have extended Calvary's benefits to all without requiring any more or greater sacrifice from Christ. It is really a play on words to say the death of Christ was *sufficient* for all but *efficient* only for those who believe if the sufficiency has already been prescribed in its extent by God. In the limited concept the sufficiency cannot, because of divine decree, exceed or go beyond the efficiency of Christ's death. Moderate Calvinists, quite to the contrary, believe that the sufficiency of the work of Christ not only could have extended to all men but that by the express design of God the Father it did extend beyond the elect. This the limited redemptionists will not admit is the teaching of Scripture and thus they should not obscure their real view by the semantic obscurity which this phrase, "sufficient for all, efficient for those who believe," really produces, since it in no way alters the limited nature of their view.

There is another phrase used by strict Calvinists which is supposed to answer objections to their limited view of the atonement. It is found frequently in attempts to explain such universal words as "all," "whosoever" and "every man." When these words are used with reference to Christ's death, limited redemptionists often say, "Christ died for all without distinction but not for all without exception." Such a statement in no way relieves the difficulties of the limited view nor does it satisfy the Biblical descriptions of the extent of the Savior's sacrifice on Calvary. Such an attempt is merely a play on words which camouflages the glaring contradiction produced when a restriction is placed on words which naturally and normally are universal in meaning.

---

[19] Steele and Thomas, *op. cit.*, p. 39.

A word of summation of the Arminian and Calvinistic views of the divine purpose of Christ's death is now in order.

The divine purpose in the Arminian view was to obtain redemption and the forgiveness of sins for all men by supplying sufficient grace to all men to believe if they will. The Calvinistic answer to the question, "Why did Christ die?" has been very much to the contrary. Calvinists who accept limited atonement believe the Savior died for the elect only and that by His death He not only provided salvation for that limited number but also infallibly secured their salvation—saved them.

IV. *The Moderate Calvinistic Answer*

Isaac Watts stated clearly the conflict between the two opposing schools of interpretation just discussed in answer to the question of the divine design of the atonement: "When the remonstrants assert that Christ died for all mankind merely to purchase conditional salvation for them; and when those who profess to be the strictest Calvinists assert [that] Christ died only to procure absolute and effectual salvation for the elect; it is not because the whole Scripture asserts the particular sentiments of either of these sects with an exclusion of the other. But the reason of these different assertions of men is this, that the holy writers in different texts pursuing different subjects, and speaking to different persons, sometimes seem to favor each of these two opinions; and men, being at a loss to reconcile them by any medium, run into different extremes, and entirely follow one of these tracks of thought and neglect the other."[20]

On the basis of what we discovered previously concerning the purpose of Christ's death, it may be emphasized again that according to Scripture Christ's death was a complete and final substitute for sinners and was most certainly designed to secure the eternal salvation of the sinner who does nothing but believe in Jesus Christ as his Savior. We observed that Scripture broadens the design of the atonement so as to include all men in a provisional way. That is, the benefits of Calvary are realized

---

[20] Isaac Watts, *Works*, VI, pp. 286, 287, cited by Jonathan Edwards and others, *The Atonement* (Boston: Congregational Board of Publication, 1859), pp. 251, 252.

and *applied* only to those who believe, but the *provision* reached to every member of Adam's race. This is the uniform testimony of Scripture and especially of those central passages such as 2 Peter 2:1, 1 John 2:2, Romans 5 and 2 Corinthians 5, which deal respectively with the limited and unlimited sense of redemption, propitiation and reconciliation.

The Godhead will surely effect all that was designed in the atonement. The question, therefore, is not, "Will the divine design be realized?" for that question is answered in the affirmative by virtue of the fact that the design is God's. Rather, the question is, "What is the divine design?" Arminians see the design of God in the atonement as the *obtaining* or *purchasing* of redemption and sufficient grace for all men, leaving man with the decision to choose or not to choose this redemption. Calvinists, of the strict type, view the design of the atonement as that which *secures* the redemption, not of all men indiscriminately, but of the elect only. So that while the Arminians and Calvinists view the design of the atonement similarly, they view the extent very differently.

The moderate Calvinist view which we are seeking to present in these pages lies between these two. Christ most certainly died to secure the salvation of those who believe—the elect—and it is our conviction that the Bible teaches that Christ died to provide a basis of salvation for all men. To those who are the elect and who therefore believe in Christ, this provision secures for them their eternal salvation, when they believe. For those who do not believe and thus evidence the fact that they are the nonelect, the provision exists as a basis of condemnation. The eternal destiny of men, according to the Bible, is not determined by the extent of the atonement or by man's relationship to Adam and his sin, but by man's relationship to Jesus Christ Who died for sin and sins—the root and the fruit (Rom. 6:10; 1 Cor. 15:3).

We, therefore, reject the idea that Christ died to *secure* the salvation of all men or that He provided every man with sufficient grace to cooperate with God. If that be true, God is defeated because all men will not be saved. We also reject the idea that Christ died to secure the salvation of the elect only. If that be true the cross can no longer be the basis of condemnation for those who do not believe (John 3:18). We believe rather that the twofold testimony of Scripture can be harmonized only in the view that believes Christ died to make possible the salvation of all men and to make certain the salvation of those who believe.

Strict Calvinists have not allowed for this mediating, and we believe Biblical, position (it is a mediating position not because it is partly Biblical and partly non-Biblical but because it is between the strict Calvinist and strict Arminian views). Usually Calvinists view the choice as either the Arminian view of providing salvation and sufficient grace for all and securing it for none or the strict Calvinistic view of securing salvation only for the elect.

A. A. Hodge speaks as though there were only two choices: "Did Christ die with the design and effect of making the salvation of all men indifferently possible, and the salvation of none certain; or did he die in pursuance of an eternal covenant between the Father and himself for the purpose as well as with the result of effecting the salvation of his own people?"[21] We must reject both of these views because neither one of them is altogether Biblical. Christ did die for all men (John 3:16; 2 Cor. 5:19; 2 Pet. 2:1; 1 John 2:2) and He also died to secure and make certain the salvation of His own (John 10:15; Eph. 5:25).

There are difficulties in harmonizing Scripture with the Arminian and the Calvinistic concepts. The fact is that Scripture does teach a total inability of man to move toward God. It denies any ability in man, whether it be called sufficient grace or something else, to respond to God and in this regard the Arminian concept is unscriptural and totally unacceptable. On the other hand, the strict Calvinistic position, which insists that Christ's death of itself saves the elect, makes faith, the sole Biblical condition of salvation, virtually unnecessary.

Another difficulty facing both of these views relates to the matter of imputation. Arminianism, because of its acceptance of the governmental theory of the atonement, objects to the im-

---

[21] Archibald Alexander Hodge, *The Atonement* (Grand Rapids: Wm. B. Eerdmans Publishing Co., 1953), p. 363.

putation of the sin of the race to Christ. So does strict Calvinism object to this same imputation or putting over to Christ's account the totality of the sin of the race, and for a similar reason. Arminians fear this truth because they believe it would lead to universalism. Calvinists reject it for the same reason and also because this would mean Christ's death was unlimited.

The fact is, the Bible teaches very clearly that Adam's sin was imputed to the race (Rom. 5:12-20), that the sin of the race was imputed or reckoned over to Christ (Isa. 53:5, 6, 11; 1 Pet. 3:18; 1 Pet. 2:24, 25; 2 Cor. 5:21), and that the righteousness of Christ is imputed to the believing sinner (Rom. 3:21, 22; 2 Cor. 5:21; Heb. 10:14).

The Arminian solution to the problem is to ascribe to all men sufficient grace enabling them to believe. The Calvinistic solution is to restrict the extent of the atonement to the elect and make it the only saving instrumentality. Neither of these solutions is completely Biblical.

Would it not be better to face Scripture objectively, accepting not only its clear teaching of man's native sinfulness and total inability to please God but also its equally clear emphasis upon the unlimited provisionary nature of the atonement and the necessary condition of faith for salvation?

The Bible is clear that man must believe to be saved. All men, including the elect, are lost until such time as they individually and personally exercise faith in Christ as their own Savior. There simply is no distinction in the Bible between elect and nonelect sinners in their unregenerate state.

The insistence of the New Testament writers upon the necessity of faith demonstrates the provisionary nature of the atonement. At least 150 times faith is made the single condition of salvation, thus stressing the fact that all the benefits of Calvary's completed work are withheld until men believe. Peter's use of one of the words for *redeem,* translated "bought" (2 Pet. 2:1), reveals that the price of redemption for all men was paid by Christ. This, of course, does not imply the release of all men; this comes only at the moment of faith in Christ.

"Certainly Christ's death of itself forgives no sinner, nor does it render unnecessary the regenerating work of the Holy Spirit.

Any one of the elect whose salvation is predetermined, and for whom Christ died, may live the major portion of his life in open rebellion against God and, during that time, manifest every feature of depravity and spiritual death. This alone should prove that men are not severally saved by the act of Christ in dying, but rather that they are saved by the divine *application* of that value when they believe. The blood of the passover lamb became efficacious only when applied to the door post."[22]

In all fairness it should be said that most limited redemptionists do not rule out the necessity of faith. Nevertheless, their strong emphasis upon Christ securing the salvation and even saving the elect in His death and at the time of His death makes the condition of faith for salvation seem rather unnecessary. This difficulty is frequently answered by limited redemptionists by their further insistence that Christ not only died for the elect, securing their salvation and saving them, but that He also procured at the same time the means whereby this salvation would be applied. That is, He purchased the necessary faith of the elect also, giving it to them as a gift which they in turn are to give back to Him at the point of salvation.

Very seldom is an attempt made to prove from Scripture that this is true; it is rather a very widespread assumption on the part of strict Calvinists. Even though Calvinistic arguments defending this matter of faith as a special gift to the elect are wanting, reference is usually made to Ephesians 2:8, 9 as a proof text: "For by grace are ye saved through faith; and that not of yourselves: it is the gift of God: Not of works, lest any man should boast."

Careful examination will reveal that this verse does not teach what some Calvinists would like it to teach. That which is "the gift of God" in the verse is not faith or grace but the entire act of salvation. This view has the support of the Greek text since the relative pronoun *that* is in the neuter gender while the word *faith* is feminine. Too, the context supports this view since the emphasis is upon salvation by grace and not by works.

---

[22] Lewis Sperry Chafer, *Systematic Theology* (Dallas: Dallas Seminary Press, 1950), III, p. 193.

Eadie, the Greek exegete, rightfully points out that Calvin himself held to salvation as the gift and not faith from this passage. Eadie's own interpretation is very clear: "The phrase *ouk ex ergon* must have salvation and not faith as its reference."[23] Many other exegetes share this view and insist upon it. As another example, Sir Robert Anderson's word will serve very well: "Eph. 2:8. 'The gift of God' here is *salvation by grace through faith*. Not the faith itself. 'This is precluded,' as Alford remarks, 'by the manifestly parallel clauses "not of yourselves," and "not of works," the latter of which would be irrelevant as asserted of faith.' "[24]

Some acknowledge that saving faith is not the special gift of God in this verse; yet they insist that it is said to be such elsewhere in Scripture. Aldrich cites the following verses as those usually used to prove the strict Calvinistic point of view: Acts 5:31; 11:18; Philippians 1:29; 3:9; Romans 12:3; 2 Peter 1:1; 2 Timothy 2:25 and John 6:44, 45. Since it is not our purpose here to refute the Calvinistic doctrine of the origin of faith, the reader is referred to the article cited above for Dr. Aldrich's very fine refutation of this Calvinistic unproven assumption. His conclusion is that while many New Testament passages and even whole books were written to prove that salvation is a gift, none of these passages or any others make faith itself the gift from God to the elect.

Calvinists believe so strongly in this that many of them arrive at a very logical conclusion if their premise be accepted. That is, faith becomes a product of regeneration and not an actual means of receiving it. Berkhof puts it this way: "This faith is not first of all an activity of man, but a potentiality wrought by God in the heart of the sinner. The seed of faith is implanted in man in regeneration."[25] Shedd makes a similar observation: "The Calvinist maintains that faith is wholly from

---

[23] John Eadie, *Commentary on the Epistle to the Ephesians* (Grand Rapids: Zondervan Publishing House, n.d.), p. 152.

[24] Sir Robert Anderson cited by Roy L. Aldrich, "The Gift of God," *Bibliotheca Sacra*, CXXII (July-September, 1965), p. 249. This is an excellent article dealing with this whole issue. It is recommended very highly.

[25] L. Berkhof, *Systematic Theology* (Grand Rapids: Wm. B. Eerdmans Publishing Co., 1953), p. 503.

God, being one of the effects of regeneration."[26] Along this same line Arthur W. Pink, a staunch Calvinist, comes up with a rather strange solution. He begins by admitting that the nonelect are *unable* to believe and then proceeds to enumerate what they must do: ". . . Set to his seal that God is true. . . . Cry unto God for His enabling power—to ask God in mercy to overcome his enmity, and 'draw' him to Christ; to bestow upon him the gifts of repentance and faith."[27] However one looks at this list of duties, it constitutes rather strenuous chores for a depraved man who it was said could not respond to the gospel in faith because he is dead in sin. As Aldrich so aptly stated it, "The extreme Calvinist deals with a rather lively spiritual corpse after all."[28]

What is the solution to this seemingly hopeless dilemma? Is there not some way to harmonize what the Bible says about the extent of the atonement, man's lost condition, God's electing purposes and the need to meet the God-ordained requirement of faith for salvation? A step in the right direction toward the understanding of these truths lies in the acceptance of certain guiding principles set forth in the Bible. All too often this problem of the relationship of God's requirement of faith for salvation with His electing purposes has been approached by assuming either the Arminian or Calvinistic view and then forcing the scriptural teaching into the mold. Here, as everywhere else, we must allow the Bible to speak for itself even if it does run counter to our previously-conceived ideas. Our first interest must never be to defend a system of theology but to understand and rightly interpret the Word of God. Here, then, are some guiding principles which will aid in the solution of the problem before us.

First, the Bible views all men as spiritually lost and sinners unable to do anything to please God. From God's perspective "there is none righteous, no, not [so much as even] one." No distinction is made between lost sinners who are elect and those who are not elect. Elect people are just as depraved as the non-

---

[26] W. G. T. Shedd, *Systematic Theology* (Grand Rapids: Zondervan Publishing House, n.d.), II, p. 472.

[27] Arthur W. Pink, *The Sovereignty of God* (Cleveland: Cleveland Bible Truth Depot, 1930), pp. 198, 199.

[28] Aldrich, *op. cit.,* p. 248.

elect. This sinful condition brought forth the wrath of God. It was not just His wrath against the sin of the elect which made necessary Christ's death but rather His wrath against every member of Adam's race. It seems to follow then that the price paid to bring divine satisfaction must be as all-inclusive and extensive as the wrath of God and the sin of man which made the satisfaction necessary in the first place.

Second, Scripture makes personal faith the sole condition for the appropriation of Calvary's benefits to the individual. Faith is commanded of all men without any distinction between the elect and nonelect, or those for whom Christ died or did not die. Also, the consequences of failing to believe or of rejecting God's provision in Christ are clearly revealed. Men are condemned for not believing in the name of the only begotten Son of God. It is true not only of those who have heard the gospel of Christ, but also of those who have not heard. God makes no difference as far as eternal destiny is concerned between those who have heard and rejected and those who have not heard of Christ but have rejected the knowledge God gave to all men of Himself in nature and the conscience (Psa. 19; Rom. 1). To reject the lesser revelation of God in nature and conscience is to reject the greater, saving revelation of God in Christ. God commands faith and repentance of all men indiscriminately (i.e., Acts 17:30), and every universal offer of the gospel and exhortation to believe must be viewed as a genuine offer from God.

The scriptural teaching of the universal necessity of personal faith for salvation does not militate against the scriptural teaching of total depravity. Men are not merely spiritually sick and in need of divine medication; they are dead and in need of divine life (Eph. 2:1, 2). Obviously, the Bible views faith or belief as a separate thing in relation to salvation. Scripture does not teach that faith follows regeneration as some Calvinists would have it. Always in the Bible men are exhorted to believe in order that they might receive life. It is never the other way around. The message of the gospel is not to regenerated people to believe in something they already have, but to believe so that they might receive what they do not have but so desperately need.

Murray, who accepts and defends limited atonement and also believes regeneration precedes faith, seems to present a contradiction when explaining the relation of faith to salvation. Beginning his chapter on faith and repentance he says, "Without regeneration it is morally and spiritually impossible for a person to believe in Christ, but when a person is regenerated it is morally and spiritually impossible for that person not to believe."[29] In words which are almost diametrically opposed to these Murray adds, "We entrust ourselves to him not because we believe we have been saved but as lost sinners in order that we may be saved."[30] How it is possible to be regenerated, to possess divine life, before the exercise of faith and not be saved is not explained by Murray.

It is better to view the aspects of the salvation process as simultaneous rather than to force the Scripture into a preconceived theological mold which in reality makes faith virtually unnecessary. "The normal pattern for regeneration is that it occurs at the moment of saving faith. No appeal is ever addressed to men that they should believe because they are already regenerated. It is rather that they should believe and receive eternal life. Christians are definitely told that before they accepted Christ they were 'dead in trespasses and sin' (Eph. 2:1, A.V.)."[31]

Third, not one sinner, though commanded of God to believe in Christ as Savior for salvation or suffer the consequences, will be saved unless and until the Holy Spirit brings him to the conviction of his sin and the realization of his need of Christ. The Lord made this very clear when He said, "No man can come to me, except the Father which hath sent me draw him . . ." (John 6:44).

Here, in clear and simple words, we have the twofold truth concerning salvation in Christ—the sinner must come; yet he will not come unless drawn by the Father. To come to Christ is the same as to believe on Him. This the Savior made explicit when in the same context He said, ". . . He that cometh to me

[29] Murray, *Redemption—Accomplished and Applied*, p. 133.
[30] *Ibid.*, pp. 136, 137.
[31] John F. Walvoord, *The Holy Spirit* (Findlay, Ohio: Dunham Publishing Company, 1958), p. 135.

shall never hunger; and he that believeth on me shall never
thirst" (John 6:35). Or again He said, "All that the Father
giveth me shall come to me; and him that cometh to me I will
in no wise cast out" (John 6:37). "And this is the will of him
that sent me, that every one which seeth the Son, and believeth
on him, may have everlasting life: and I will raise him up at
the last day" (John 6:40).

Mysterious as it may seem to us, the fact remains that men
must come or believe to be saved, and yet they will not have
the desire or the ability to come unless and until they are drawn
by God to do so. The natural man, the unsaved man, simply
does not possess the ability to receive the things of the Spirit of
God. They are foolishness to him, and he cannot know them (1
Cor. 2:14). Unsaved men have a darkened understanding, and
they are alienated from God (Eph. 4:18). Their minds are at
enmity with God (Rom. 8:7) and are blinded by Satan (2 Cor.
4:4). Therefore, before a man can or will ever come to Christ,
the Spirit of God must effectually call him, show him his sin, his
need of God's righteousness in Christ, and bring him to faith in
Christ as Savior.

It is true that common grace or the Spirit's general work of
restraining sin (Gen. 6:3; 2 Thess. 2:7) and His general conviction of the world (John 16:8-11) reveals man's need of salvation; yet it falls short of the actual salvation of the individual.
Man in his lost condition requires more than an understanding
of his need; he needs divine enablement and this comes through
efficacious or special grace at the precise moment of faith, being
simultaneous with it. The Bible relates these two very closely—
the Spirit's work of giving life and the individual's reception of
it by faith. The one is never seen without the other.

"If one accepts the Biblical revelation of man's state of spiritual death and total inability, he must accept the doctrine of
efficacious grace as the solution to the problem. . . . The Scriptures, however, give adequate witness both to the fact of the effectual call and to the human responsibility to believe in
Christ. . . . While in the experience of the individual, faith in
Christ is a result of choice, an act of the human will, it is
nevertheless a work of efficacious grace. Efficacious grace never

operates in a heart that is still rebellious, and no one is ever saved against his will."[32]

Fourth, this faith in Christ as Savior which is necessary for salvation does not add anything to the full and complete redemption procured by Christ. Faith does not save; Christ saves and Christ alone. Faith must be viewed as a means through which the grace of God comes to the needy heart. The salvation received is not improved upon nor is its nature altered in any way by the reception of it by faith.

Fifth, Scripture declares that faith is not a work. "But to him that worketh not, but believeth on him that justifieth the ungodly, his faith is counted for righteousness" (Rom. 4:5). Faith in the Scriptures is never spoken of as God's faith, but it is always associated with man. Men are required to exercise faith, and this in no sense implies gaining merit or earning salvation since the Bible itself makes faith the condition of receiving the free, undeserved and unearned grace—salvation. Long ago, Gresham Machen said, ". . . Faith consists not in doing something but in receiving something."[33] Another Calvinist joins in distinguishing faith from any good work: "Faith is no more than an activity of reception contributing nothing to that which it receives."[34]

Conclusion

An attempt has been made in this chapter to answer the question, "Why did Christ die?"

The answer from Arminianism is that He died to obtain redemption and forgiveness of sins for all men, thus giving to all sufficient grace to cooperate with God for salvation. This view must be rejected in view of the scriptural teaching of man's total inability and total lack of merit before God. To say all men possess sufficient grace to be saved if they will flatly contradicts the Bible's testimony of the unsaved man's natural condition.

[32] *Ibid.,* pp. 123-125.
[33] J. Gresham Machen, *What is Faith?* (Grand Rapids: Wm. B. Eerdmans Publishing Co., 1925), p. 172.
[34] J. I. Packer, *Fundamentalism and the Word of God* (Grand Rapids: Wm. B. Eerdmans Publishing Co., 1960), p. 172.

Strict Calvinism, we have seen, replies to the question by stressing Christ's death as a substitute for elect sinners only, a substitute which includes the procuring of the faith necessary for the salvation of those elect sinners. Strict Calvinists believe the cross secures its own benefits—the cross saves. This seems to minimize the necessity of faith since Christ's salvation is not potential but actual for the elect. It also means that the sin of the race was not imputed to Christ but only the sins of the elect.

Moderate Calvinists acknowledge and accept fully the vicarious substitutionary nature of the atonement but they insist that the Bible makes that full and complete sacrifice provisionary. They believe the cross does not apply its own benefits but that God has conditioned His full and free salvation upon personal faith in order to appropriate its accomplishments to the individual. This faith which men must exercise is not a work whereby man contributes his part to his salvation. Nor does faith, in the moderate Calvinist view, improve in any way the final and complete sacrifice of Calvary. It is simply the method of applying Calvary's benefits which the sovereign God has deigned to use in His all-wise plan of salvation.

For the moderate Calvinist, therefore, the basis upon which men will be eternally lost is not only their sin in Adam but also because of their rejection of the provision of salvation for them in Christ. To the believer the cross becomes his means of salvation when he believes, and to the unbeliever it remains a basis of condemnation until he does believe.

What a sovereign God is ours Who could devise a plan of salvation so infinite and complete! This divine plan, formulated before the foundations of the world, included Christ's death as a substitute for all, the Spirit's work of conviction and the necessity of faith for the application and appropriation of that completed work.

He left His Father's throne above,
So free, so infinite His grace!
Emptied Himself of all but love,
And bled for Adam's helpless race.

Amazing love! How can it be
That Thou, my God, shouldst die for me?
Amazing love! How can it be
That Thou, my God, shouldst die for me?

—*Charles Wesley*

III

THE BIBLICAL EXTENT OF
THE ATONEMENT

In the previous chapter we concluded that the purpose of the Father in the death of His Son was to provide salvation for all. Taking into account the Biblical evidence for man's total inability, the need of the Holy Spirit's work in the sinner's heart and the necessity of personal faith in Christ for the appropriation of salvation, this seems to be a scriptural conclusion.

We now come to a second question, "For whom did Christ die?" As was indicated earlier, the nature and purpose of His death determines the extent of His death. Since we have said He died as a final and complete substitute, providing salvation for Adam's race, the case would seem to be closed. However, our purpose here is to examine the scriptural evidence on both sides of the question. In this process it will be necessary for us to divorce ourselves as much as possible from any preconceived viewpoints.

I. *Scripture Which Limits the Extent of the Atonement* (italics all mine)

Isaiah 53:5: "But he was wounded for *our* transgressions, he was bruised for *our* iniquities: the chastisement of *our* peace was upon him; and with his stripes *we* are healed." Without question, Christ the Messiah is the one in view here Who was to be wounded and bruised for men. It is equally clear that Isaiah is speaking about his own people, the Jews, in the personal pronouns. Thus, the most ardent limited redemptionist must admit that this limited passage is too limited inasmuch as some Gentiles were saved, although Isaiah speaks of the Jews nationally.

Matthew 1:21: ". . . For he shall save *his people* from their sins." That Christ would relate His salvation to "his people" is very clear. It seems equally clear in the context that Christ was coming to save His own race—the Jewish race. The recorded genealogy, Christ's association with David and the fulfillment of Hebrew prophecy all point to the Jews. However, even the most ardent limited redemptionist surely would not want to extend the benefits of Christ's death to the Jews only. Even this "limited" passage must then be broadened to include at least some Gentiles.

Matthew 20:28: "Even as the Son of man came not to be ministered unto, but to minister, and to give his life a ransom *for many*." The preposition translated "for" clearly teaches substitution—one in the place of another.

Matthew 26:28: "For this is my blood of the new testament, which is shed *for many* for the remission of sins." Though a different preposition is used here which sometimes means "for the benefit of," substitution is nevertheless plainly in view.

John 10:15: ". . . I lay down my life *for the sheep*."

Galatians 3:13: "Christ hath redeemed *us* from the curse of the law, being made a curse *for us*. . . ." Obviously, Paul is speaking in the context to believers; and since he includes himself here, he is relating the redemption to the redeemed. The question here, as in many other instances where writers of Scripture include themselves when speaking of the death of Christ, is, "Does this mean the writer is excluding all others except believers?" How else could Paul have related Christ's death to himself without saying He died for "us"? If references such as this, in which the writer includes himself in the death of Christ, may be used to prove limited atonement, then when writers of Scripture use similar phraseology in speaking of man's sin, it could be said that they teach limited depravity or sin. For example, in such passages as, "the LORD hath laid on him the iniquity of *us* all" or "all *our* righteousnesses are as filthy rags," are we to understand by the writer's inclusion of himself that thereby only believers are sinners? On the basis of such an argument it could also be said that God loves only believers since John says, "We love him, because he first loved *us*." Surely, that John includes himself and other believers in God's love does not mean God does not love unbelievers, though many limited redemptionists affirm that to be the case.

The curse spoken of in the Galatians 3 context extends to "every one that continueth not in all things which are written in the book of the law to do them" (Gal. 3:10). The curse is as far-reaching as the fall since no one is justified by keeping the law (Gal. 3:11). Now, the point of verse 13 is that Christ's death reached to those under the curse (all men) and delivered them from it by becoming a curse in their stead. Of course, that deliverance was a living reality for the apostle because he had personally appropriated it by faith, but does the fact that he says it is true of himself and other believers mean the same deliverance was not provided for all the others who were under the curse?

Morris summarizes the meaning of the passage very well: "How, then, does Paul conceive of Christ's removing the curse from men? Christ, he says, became a curse for us, and this is linked with a curse pronounced by the law on 'everyone that hangeth upon a tree.' A curse rests on everyone who does not fulfill the law; Christ died in such a way as to bear or be a curse; we who should have been accursed now go free."[1]

Ephesians 5:25: ". . . Christ also loved the *church,* and gave himself *for it.*" Unless the church is made to refer to the saints of all ages (which cannot be done without departing from a literal interpretation; cf. Matt. 16:18; 1 Cor. 10:32; Heb. 12:22, 23), this passage must also be extended beyond the borders of that new entity established on the day of Pentecost (Acts 2). No one who believes Israel and the church are distinct and entire-

---

[1] Leon Morris, *The Apostolic Preaching of the Cross* (Grand Rapids: Wm. B. Eerdmans Publishing Co., 1956), p. 53.

ly separate can appeal to this passage in Ephesians 5 to support the limited redemptionist view. Certainly Christ died for others outside of the body of Christ.

Hebrews 9:28: "So Christ was once offered to bear the *sins of many. . . .*"

Acts 20:28: "Take heed therefore unto yourselves, and to all the flock . . . to feed *the church of God, which he hath purchased with his own blood.*" The word translated "purchased" in this text means to "preserve one's life" as in Luke 17:33. "In contrast to the use of *agorazo,* which would emphasize the idea of purchase, the verb used here has more the thought of the result of the action, that the church has been 'acquired.' The idea is therefore one of possession rather than emphasis on the act of purchase."[2]

These selected passages serve to illustrate the fact that the Bible does speak of the atonement in relation to specific individuals and groups. According to these and other passages, Christ came to redeem His own, to provide a ransom for many, to die for the sheep and to give Himself for the church. And the unlimited redemptionist has absolutely no problem reconciling all such references with his view. It should be understood, however, that none of the passages which speak of Christ's death for specific groups or individuals can be used to exclude others. This is true since they only tell us of a certain group for whom Christ did die, and they do not tell us that He did not die for others. In other words, nowhere in Scripture does it ever say Christ did not die for all men.

II. *Scripture Which Broadens the Extent of the Atonement to Include All Men (italics all mine)*

A. *Passages Containing the Word "World"*

Although many passages fall into this category, only a few will be cited here.

John 1:29: ". . . Behold the Lamb of God, which taketh away the sin of *the world.*"

John 3:16: "For God so loved *the world. . . .*" "In this pas-

---

[2] John F. Walvoord, "Redemption," *Bibliotheca Sacra,* CXIX (January-March, 1962), pp. 6, 7.

sage, as almost no other, a restricted use of the term *cosmos* is presented; not restricted, as the Limited Redemptionist demands, to the elect of this age, but restricted to humanity itself apart from its evil institutions, practices, and relationships. God loved the lost people who make up the *cosmos* and this love was great enough to move Him to give His only begotten Son, in providing a way of salvation through Him so complete that by believing on the Son as Savior the lost of this *cosmos* might not perish but have everlasting life.''[3]

A seeming paradox appears in the light of this truth of God's love for the world with the clear exhortation in Scripture to the believer to "Love not the world, neither the things that are in the world . . ." (1 John 2:15). God loves the world; and yet, if the believer loves it, God's love is not in him. The solution to this problem is to be found in the obvious meaning of the "world" in each case. God loved the world of men and proved it by giving His Son; the believer is to reciprocate that love for God and lost men by not loving the evil world-system because it is headed by Satan (John 12:31; Eph. 2:2; 2 Cor. 4:4).

John 3:17: "For God sent not his Son into the world to condemn the world; but that *the world through him might be saved.*"

John 4:42: ". . . This is indeed the Christ, the Saviour of *the world.*"

Second Corinthians 5:19: "To wit, that God was in Christ, reconciling *the world* unto himself. . . ."

First John 4:14: ". . . The Father sent the Son to be the Saviour of the world.*"

B. *Passages Containing the Word "Whosoever"*

Chafer observes that "the word *whosoever* is used at least 110 times in the New Testament, and always with the unrestricted meaning."[4] This being the case, the following have been selected as examples:

John 3:16: ". . . That *whosoever believeth* in him should not perish, but have everlasting life."

---

[3] Lewis Sperry Chafer, *Systematic Theology* (Dallas: Dallas Seminary Press, 1950), II, p. 78.
[4] *Ibid.*, III, p. 204.

Acts 2:21: ". . . *Whosoever shall call* on the name of the Lord shall be saved."

Acts 10:43: ". . . Through his name *whosoever believeth* in him shall receive remission of sins."

Romans 10:13: "For *whosoever shall call* upon the name of the Lord shall be saved."

Revelation 22:17: ". . . And *whosoever will,* let him take the water of life freely."

C. *Passages Containing the Word "All" or Its Equivalent*

Again, only a few of the many passages will be cited.

Luke 19:10: "For the Son of man is come to seek and to save *that which was lost."*

Romans 5:6: ". . . Christ died for the *ungodly."*

First Timothy 2:6: "Who gave himself *a ransom for all,* to be testified in due time." This verse contains a word here translated "ransom" which does not occur anywhere else in the New Testament. The word was formed by the prefixed preposition *anti,* which clearly teaches substitution, to the simple word *lutron,* which means "ransom" or "release." Concerning the use of this rare word formed by these two other words, Morris says: "Such a term well suits the context, for we read of Christ 'who gave himself on behalf of all' (1 Tim. 2:6). The thought clearly resembles that of Mk. x.45, i.e., that Jesus has died in the stead of those who deserved death. If the thought of substitution is there, we find it here to an even greater degree in view of the addition of the preposition which emphasizes substitution."[5]

Second Corinthians 5:14, 15: ". . . That if one died *for all,* then were *all dead:* And that he died *for all,* that they which live should not henceforth live unto themselves, but unto him which died for them, and rose again." Building a background for his doctrine of reconciliation in this passage, Paul begins with the love of Christ which eventuated in His death for all, which in turn resulted in the death of all (v. 14). There can be no doubt that substitution is in view here just as it is in Matthew 20:28 and Mark 10:45 where Christ is said to give His life a

---

[5] Morris, *op. cit.,* p. 48.

"ransom for many."[6] Morris puts it this way: "One died, not many. But the death of that one means that the many died. If language has meaning, this surely signifies that the death of the One took the place of the death of the many."[7] ". . . He died that death which is the death of all."[8] "The thought is that when Christ died the sinner died."[9]

The verses under consideration (2 Cor. 5:14, 15) provide strong argument for the universality of the atonement. Making the word "all" in these verses refer to the elect only, which is what the limited redemptionist is forced to do, leads to a meaningless interpretation. What would happen to the *elect* in verse 15 who did not "live"?

Attitudes and feelings toward men in general are changed in those who "live" or have appropriated the death of Christ. The love of Christ for the world of men which led to His death for them (v. 14) means that the believer's entire outlook on people has undergone a change. Men are no longer to be viewed "after the flesh" or in a "fleshly way" (v. 16). They are now to be viewed as those for whom Christ died.

Walvoord's summarization of these verses is pertinent. "This concept of the universality of the provision of reconciliation is borne out in the context, in which reconciliation is discussed. In 2 Corinthians 5:14, emphasis is given to the fact that all were dead spiritually. The three instances of 'all' in 2 Corinthians 5:14-15 seem to be universal. This is followed by the limited application indicated in the phrase 'they which live.' Hence, the passage reads: 'For the love of Christ constraineth us; because we thus judge, that one died for all [universal], therefore all [universal] died; and he died for all [universal], that they that live [restricted to elect] shall no longer live unto themselves,

---

[6] *Huper* is so used with the clear meaning of *anti* in Philemon 13 and in the papyri. Compare R. C. H. Lenski, *The Interpretation of St. Paul's First and Second Epistle to the Corinthians* (Columbus: Wartburg Press, 1946), pp. 1029, 1030; and Richard Chenevix Trench, *Synonyms of the New Testament* (Grand Rapids: Wm. B. Eerdmans Publishing Co., 1953), pp. 310-313.

[7] Leon Morris, *The Cross in the New Testament* (Grand Rapids: Wm. B. Eerdmans Publishing Co., 1965), p. 220.

[8] *Ibid.*, p. 239.

[9] *Ibid.*, p. 380.

but unto him who for their sakes died and rose again' (2 Cor. 5:14-15). The word 'all' is used, then, in a universal sense in this passage, followed by the restricted application indicated in the phrase, 'they which live.' This is reinforced by the use of the word 'world,' referring to all men, in verse 19."[10]

Those determined to make Scripture conform to the five-point Calvinistic mold must, out of necessity, reduce the "all" here, as elsewhere, to "some" or the "elect." John Owen, for example, insists that both of the "alls" in verse 14 are of equal extent. Owen says Paul does "not say, that 'Christ died for all that were dead,' but only, that 'all were dead which Christ died for': which proves no more but this, that all they whom Christ died for, were dead, with that kind of death, of which he speaks. The extent of the words, is to be taken from the first *all,* and not the latter. The apostle affirms, so many to be dead, as Christ died for, not that Christ died for so many as were dead."[11] Without doubt, this is a typical strict Calvinistic explanation of this clear passage. No wonder someone exclaimed, "The Calvinistic efforts to limit this word to 'all the elect' constitute one of the saddest chapters in exegesis. The Scriptures shine with the 'all' of universality, but Calvinists do not see it. Their one effort is to find something that would justify them to reduce 'all' to 'some.' Calvin himself says that all = all kinds, all classes, taking *some* of each, but *not all* in the sense of every individual."[12]

When the great emphasis in Scripture upon the necessity of faith is omitted, and even in this very passage if the clear distinction between the "all" for whom Christ died and "they which live" be overlooked, the Calvinistic charge of universalism against those who believe "all" here means every individual would be valid. Such a charge lacks validity, however, since Paul is speaking of the provision of Christ and not the securing of salvation.

---

[10] John F. Walvoord, "Reconciliation," *Bibliotheca Sacra*, CXX (January-March, 1963), p. 10.
[11] John Owen, *The Works of John Owen,* ed. Thomas Cloutt (London: J. F. Dove, 1823), V, p. 465.
[12] Lenski, *op. cit.,* p. 1029.

Titus 2:11: "For the grace of God that bringeth salvation *hath appeared to all men.*"

Hebrews 2:9: ". . . That he by the grace of God should taste *death for every man.*"

Second Peter 3:9: "The Lord is . . . not willing that any should perish, but that *all should come* to repentance."

First Timothy 4:10: ". . . We trust in the living God, who is the *Saviour of all men,* specially of those that believe."

D. Limited Redemptionist's Explanation of the Unlimited Passages

Those who are strict Calvinists, and therefore believe in limited atonement, are not unaware of the passages of Scripture which seem to teach an unlimited redemption. Neither have they failed to offer some explanations of them, even though their explanations are usually rather brief and superficial.

That host of passages including the words "all," "whosoever" and "world" is frequently dismissed in the following manner: "One reason for the use of these expressions was to correct the false notion that salvation was for the Jews alone. Such phrases as 'the world,' 'all men,' 'all nations,' and 'every creature' were used by the New Testament writers to emphatically correct this mistake. These expressions are intended to show that Christ died for all men without *distinction* (i.e., He died for Jews and Gentiles alike) but they are not intended to indicate that Christ died for all men without *exception* (i.e., He did not die for the purpose of saving each and every lost sinner)."[13]

We must agree with this last observation and do so gladly. Christ did not die to save every lost sinner, and if He did, He was defeated; for they are not all saved. He did die, though, *to make possible* the salvation of every lost sinner, to make them all savable, and that is saying something quite different from what Arminians and strict Calvinists say.

Even though Steele does not cite any references where these universal and all-inclusive phrases sometimes refer to the distinction between Jews and Gentiles, this is no doubt sometimes

[13] David N. Steele and Curtis C. Thomas, *The Five Points of Calvinism Defined, Defended, Documented* (Philadelphia: The Presbyterian and Reformed Publishing Co., 1963), p. 46.

true. However, it is equally true that this sweeping "removal" of the intention of these broad and unlimited words regarding the atonement simply does not answer the problem.

This explanation on the part of limited redemptionists does not fit all the passages. What Jew-Gentile distinction was John trying to remove in his Gospel (John 1:29; 3:16)? There is nothing in the context which would warrant saying John was trying to remove such a distinction.

One must certainly strain contexts to find such a purpose in the mind of Paul in his exhortation to Timothy (1 Tim. 2:3-6) or to Titus (Titus 2:11) or in the mind of Peter (2 Pet. 3:9). Even if such an intention to remove distinction between Jew and Gentile would be granted in these and similar passages, this still does not prove that those among the Jews and Gentiles for whom Christ died were all of the elect.

Too, what are we to do with such a broad term as "ungodly" in Romans 5:6, the "lost" in Luke 19:10 or the phrase "every man" in Hebrews 2:9? It would have been very easy for the writers of these passages to limit and confine the scope of Christ's death had that been the Spirit's intention. One must perform mental and theological gymnastics to confine these statements to the elect. The elect are not the only "ungodly" ones (Rom. 5:6), "lost" ones (Luke 19:10), nor do the elect constitute the totality of mankind (Heb. 2:9); and yet the Son is said to have died for all the ungodly, all the lost and all mankind.

Limited redemptionists have another way of interpreting these universal passages. They do it by saying there are instances in Scripture where these words (i.e., "all," "world," etc.) do not mean one hundred percent of everyone and everything. For example, Hodge cites Luke 2:1 as an example and says, "When it is said that 'a decree went out from Caesar Augustus that all the world should be taxed' (Luke 2:1), no man understands that the term 'all the world' is to be taken absolutely."[14]

Or take this example: "When Jesus predicted: 'Ye shall be hated of all men for my name's sake' (Matt. 10:22), He surely

---

[14] A. A. Hodge, *The Atonement* (Grand Rapids: Wm. B. Eerdmans Publishing Co., 1953), p. 424.

did not mean that His disciples would be hated by every single man, woman, and child in the world, but only that worldly people, constituting the great majority of men, would hate them."[15] The same writer goes on to say: "And when the Pharisees commented on Jesus' great popularity after the resurrection of Lazarus: 'Behold, the world is gone after him' (John 12:19), they were obviously using the term 'world' in a much restricted sense."[16]

Now there is certainly no question about the fact that these words are sometimes used in a restricted sense. No unlimited redemptionist would deny that fact. The question, however, is not related to the possibility of such restrictions as obviously exist in certain cases. The question is, *"Is it scripturally and logically sound always to restrict every usage of the words 'all,' 'whosoever' and 'world' when they occur in a salvation context?"* This is precisely what the limited redemptionist always does and must do. There may not be a single exception if the limited viewpoint is to stand. The basis for this restriction rests upon the fact that in some instances, which are unrelated to the work of Christ on the cross, the words are thus restricted. But is this a valid reason for always restricting them in salvation passages? We say no, and we say it emphatically. Chafer has observed how strange some of these passages sound when translated as the limited redemptionist must interpret them. " 'God so loved the elect, that He gave His only begotten Son, that whosoever [of the elect] believeth in Him should not perish, but have everlasting life.' 2 Corinthians 5:19 would read: 'God was in Christ, reconciling the elect unto Himself.' Hebrews 2:9 would read: 'He tasted death for every man of those who comprise the company of the elect.' 1 John 2:2 would read: 'He is the propitiation for our [the elect] sins: and not for our's only, but also for the sins of those who comprise the world of elect people.' John 1:29 would read: 'Behold the Lamb of God, which taketh away the sin of the elect.' "[17]

---

[15] R. B. Kuiper, *For Whom Did Christ Die?* (Grand Rapids: Wm. B. Eerdmans Publishing Co., 1959), p. 28.

[16] *Ibid.*

[17] Chafer, *op. cit.*, III, pp. 203, 204.

We might add two more: "For the Son of man came to seek and to save that which was lost [of the elect]" (Luke 19:10) and "Christ died for the ungodly [of the elect]" (Rom. 5:6). In all honesty we must ask, "Why did not these writers say what they meant? If they meant elect people, why not say that since those who will never be saved are also *lost* and *ungodly*?"

Strange words these are! The only way in which these expressions can be so interpreted is by forcing the Scripture into a strict Calvinistic mold. But the Scripture will not thus be browbeaten. Instead of Scripture referring to the elect as the "world," which would be necessary to the limited viewpoint, it is emphatic in distinguishing the elect from the world. Is not this what Christ meant when He said, "I have chosen you out of the world, therefore the world hateth you" (John 15:19)?

Added to the impossibility of thus restricting the word "world" to the world of the elect (the Scripture seems clearly to distinguish the elect from the world), are the absurdities and self-contradictions of such an interpretation.

Let us follow through with the limited view and interpretation of the word "world" in such a simple and familiar passage as John 3:16. If "world" means the elect only, then it would follow that he "of the elect" that believeth may be saved and he "of the elect" that believeth not is condemned (cf. John 3:18). This absurdity would contradict the most basic point of Calvinism, namely, that God has elected from eternity past certain individuals and that they alone will be saved. Whoever heard of elect people being damned, and yet that is precisely what the limited interpretation leads to in John 3:16-18 when the limited concept is followed through.

The problem with the limited redemptionist is that, instead of accepting the testimony of Scripture of an atonement which was provisional for all and dependent for the bestowal of its benefits upon personal appropriation by faith, he insists that the mass of universal passages must be forced into agreement with the few limited ones.

Equally strange are the interpretations given to Hebrews 2:9 and 1 Timothy 4:10 by the limited redemptionists. Contemporary limited redemptionists usually quote John Calvin or John Owen on these verses; therefore, the views of these men will be given.

Concerning the phrase, "that he by the grace of God should taste death for every man," in Hebrews 2:9, Calvin says: "By saying *for every man,* he means not only that he might be an example to others . . . but he means that Christ died for us, and that by taking upon him what was due to us, he redeemed us from the curse of death."[18] Thus, Calvin evidently assumed this reference to be confined to the elect by his use of the word "us." He did not seek to explain how this could be so in this passage. John Owen, his editor, did explain this more fully in a footnote: " 'For every man,' *huper pantos,* that is, 'man,' mentioned in verse 6; and 'man' there means all the faithful, to whom God in Noah restored the dominion lost in Adam; but this dominion was not renewed to man as a fallen being, but as made righteous by faith."[19]

In his own work Owen said of this verse: " 'Every man' . . . is put for 'all men' by an enallage of number, the singular for the plural, for all men; that is, all those many sons which God by his death intended to bring unto glory, verse 10; those sanctified by him, whom he calls his brethren, verses 11, 12 and children given him by God, verse 13; whom by death he delivers from the fear of death, verses 14, 15; even all the seed of Abraham, verse 16."[20]

This is the kind of explanation which would be expected, but it simply does not solve the problem. In the first place there is nothing in the context of this passage nor in that of Psalm 8, from which it is being quoted, to warrant saying that "man" in verse 6 means "all the faithful." Furthermore, the very fact that the writer has been dealing with the universality of the subjection in verse 8 supports the universality of the provision of redemption in verse 9. Added to this is the change from the general to the particular in the passage. The tasting of death was for every man (v. 9) but the bringing of many sons unto

---

[18] John Calvin, *Commentaries on the Epistle of Paul the Apostle to the Hebrews,* trans. and ed. John Owen (Grand Rapids: Wm. B. Eerdmans Publishing Co., 1948), p. 61.

[19] *Ibid.*

[20] Owen, *op. cit.,* Vol. XII quoted by Kuiper, *op. cit.,* pp. 28, 29.

glory (v. 10) only relates to those sanctified or set apart through faith (v. 11). Therefore, the "brethren" and "they who are sanctified" constitute a group from among the ones for whom He tasted death. This is the only natural way to explain the change from the universal to the particular.

Alford's comment relating to the singular instead of the plural here is pertinent. "If it be asked, why *pantos* rather than *panton*, we may safely say that the singular brings out, far more strongly than the plural would, the applicability of Christ's death *to each individual man. . . .*"[21] In the same vein Robertson says: "The author . . . puts Christ's death in behalf of (*huper*), and so instead of, every man as the motive for his incarnation and death on the cross."[22]

On the phrase in 1 Timothy 4:10, ". . . who is the Saviour of all men, specially of those that believe," Calvin said, ". . . for the word *soter* is here a general term, and denotes one who defends and preserves. He means that the kindness of God extends to all men."[23] Acknowledging that the term "Saviour" refers primarily to God the Father, Owen attempts therefore to remove the universal nature of this passage. He says: "Is it not the living God in whom we trust that is the Saviour here mentioned?"[24] He also argues from the fact that the word "mediator" is not used.[25]

No doubt the reference here is to God the Father since He is spoken of in the context (vv. 4, 5), though it is not impossible that the Son is here being called "the living God" since He is also mentioned in the nearer context (v. 6). Granting the limited view the benefit of the doubt, this passage still insists on a universal work and a particular work. Nicole put it this way: "The *prima facié* force of *malista* certainly is that all men share in some degree in that salvation which the *pistoi* enjoy in the

[21] Henry Alford, *The Greek Testament* (Boston: Lee and Shepard Publishers, 1874), IV, p. 41.
[22] Archibald Thomas Robertson, *Word Pictures in the New Testament* (Nashville: Broadman Press, 1932), V, p. 346.
[23] John Calvin, *Commentaries on the Epistles to Timothy, Titus, and Philemon*, trans. William Pringle (Grand Rapids: Wm. B. Eerdmans Publishing Co., 1948), p. 112.
[24] Owen, *op. cit.*, V, p. 268.
[25] *Ibid.*

highest degree. . . . The statement is more unreservedly univer-salist in tone than chap. 2.4 and Tit. 2.11; and perhaps must be qualified by saying that while God is potentially Saviour of all, He is actually Saviour of the *pistoi.*"[26]

E. Passages Dealing with Redemption, Propitiation and Reconciliation

"It is finished!" Of the seven last sayings of Christ this one provides us with the Lord's own testimony of the completeness and sufficiency of His death.

The name of Michelangelo is no doubt familiar to most people. Michelangelo was the great sculptor, designer, painter and architect. The story is told that he was very temperamental and that it took him many years to complete some of his works. Knowledge about Michelangelo's world-famous statues of Moses and David has spread far and wide. What many people do not know, however, is that in Florence, Italy, an entire hall is filled with his *unfinished* sculptural works. Great though he was, he left more work unfinished than finished.

Jesus Christ left no unfinished works. The night before Calvary's experience He said, "I have finished the work which thou gavest me to do" (John 17:4). On the cross in His dying moments there fell from His parched lips the same cry of com-pletion and absolute fulfillment, "It is finished."

What was finished? Surely Jesus need not inform God or man that His physical life was about to end. That was so obvious it need not be stated. It is equally true that the suffering, ridicule and blasphemy which He endured at the hands of men were ended. In fact, never again would He be nailed to a cross and endure the torments of hell, the weight of sin and the turned back of His Father. That and much more was all finished and never to be repeated.

Yet, there must be more involved in Christ's cry than these things. Robertson calls the words of Christ, "A cry of victory in the hour of defeat. . . ."[27] The word translated "it is finished"

[26] W. Robertson Nicole, *The Expositor's Greek Testament* (Grand Rapids: Wm. B. Eerdmans Publishing Co., 1956), IV, p. 125.
[27] Robertson, *op. cit.,* p. 304.

means to bring something to its desired end, and the form of the word used here by our Lord means it was finished in the past, it is now finished and it will remain finished in the future. The eternal plan of God for the salvation of men had now been enacted in time with the fruits of it extending into eternity future.

This announcement of victory in the hour of seeming defeat stands out in bold contrast to the oft-repeated sacrifices of the old economy in pre-cross days. No more is there any need for bloody animal sacrifices to be offered continually for priest and people; for now the supreme sacrifice had been offered to which all the others pointed. Christ as priest and sacrifice offered Himself once and for all, and His sacrifice need never be repeated. "It is finished."

Of the meaning of this phrase, Chafer has well said, "It was rather the divine announcement of the fact that a complete transaction regarding the judgment of sin and the sufficient grounds of salvation for every sinner was accomplished."[28]

There are three great words which sum up the totality of the completed work of Christ on the cross—redemption, propitiation and reconciliation. It is our purpose here to examine each of these doctrines in relation to the extent of the atonement. Biblical usage of these terms in relation to the death of Christ reveals that they are used of a select and limited group and also of the work of Christ for the whole world. What is even more significant is the fact that sometimes both the limited and unlimited concepts appear in the same passage of Scripture.

Redemption

The doctrine of redemption fills the pages of both Old and New Testaments. Though various words are used in Scripture to convey the idea of redemption, the basic meaning remains the same—freedom by the payment of a price.

Several key passages deserve our attention in an attempt to understand the Biblical extent of the redemption provided by Christ on the cross.

Second Peter 2:1: "But there were false prophets also among the people, even as there shall be *false teachers* among you,

---

[28] Lewis Sperry Chafer, *Salvation* (Wheaton: Van Kampen Press, 1947), p. 33.

who privily *shall bring in damnable heresies, even denying the Lord that bought them,* and bring upon themselves swift destruction." The word translated "bought" is from the Greek word *agorazo* which means to purchase or acquire by the paying of a ransom or price. In its classical usage the word was used of the purchase of slaves in the slave market. Here this great redeeming work of Christ extends even to false teachers who deny the Lord and thus are never saved. Interestingly enough, this same word is used in speaking of believers who are said to be purchased by Christ's death (1 Cor. 6:20; 7:23). Two things are of extreme importance in the 2 Peter passage. One is that the purchase price of redemption was paid by the Lord for even the false prophets and teachers, even though they quite obviously never accept it. The other important feature is that these for whom the purchase price was paid are heretics of the vilest sort, since they deny the only possible basis of salvation—the substitutionary atonement of Christ. They bring to the people "damnable heresies." The word translated "damnable" really means "destructive" and ". . . speaks of the loss of everything that makes human existence worthwhile."[29] These heretics not only bring to the people these destructive heresies but Peter adds, they "bring upon themselves swift destruction." This is the same word translated *damnable* earlier in the verse. In other words, these individuals, whoever they are, deny the substitutionary nature of Christ's death and thus endure eternal separation from God; yet they are the very ones for whom Christ paid the purchase price. "Having been bought by the Master, they were His and their lives should have been lived to His glory, and it is only against this background that their sin can be seen in all its vileness. There is also probably a contrast between their faithlessness and the love of Christ who paid such a price in love for them."[30]

One is reminded of another cry of the Savior while on the cross: "Father, forgive them; for they know not what they do" (Luke 23:34). To the honest observer it seems as though the

---

[29] Kenneth Wuest, *In These Last Days* (Grand Rapids: Wm. B. Eerdmans Publishing Co., 1954), p. 47.

[30] Morris, *The Apostolic Preaching of the Cross,* p. 51.

meaning of the implications of this cry is self-evident. Either the prayer was answered or it was not. If it was not, serious question is brought to bear upon the person of the Savior. If it was answered, then in accord with the rest of Scripture it means Christ's death provided the basis of forgiveness even for those who rejected Him and crucified Him. The only other alternative would be to say all of the Christ rejectors who were putting Him to death were elect people and that seems hardly possible.

Galatians 3:13: "Christ hath *redeemed us* from the curse of the law. . . ." A slightly different word is used here for "redeem." It is the same word as found in 2 Peter 2:1 with the prepositional prefix meaning "out" before it. Thus the work of redemption is here extended to the saved, since Paul includes himself, in contrast to the 2 Peter passage where it is extended to all, including the nonelect.

The additional factor here, however, is the prefixed preposition "out" to the word "redeem" which makes the meaning of the word a bit different. After the purchase price was paid for a slave, the owner would take the slave out of the marketplace. Paying the purchase price and removing the slave were two distinct acts. Thus, when Paul uses this word in relation to himself and other believers, he is saying that Christ paid the price demanded, and for the one who accepts the payment there is additional deliverance from the bondage and servitude of sin. This is not said to be true of all men; but in this context it is related only to the believer, whereas the simple word *agorazo* is used by Peter in 2:1 to apply to all men, even those who reject its efficacy.

There is a third important word in the original language, translated "redeem" in our English New Testaments, which is not used of all men indiscriminately but only of believers. This is the word *lutro* and implies that the purchased one who is taken from the slave market is ransomed or released and set free. Peter uses this word in a context related to the believer's service in 1 Peter 1:18, and Paul also uses it in relation to Christ's sacrifice for men in 1 Timothy 2:6. The believing sinner is no longer a slave in bondage to sin and Satan, but because of the acceptance of the purchased redemption he is now delivered from sin's binding fetters and, even more, is released so that he now can become a voluntary bondslave of Christ, the new Master.

The conclusion to be drawn from the New Testament usage of these three words for "redeem" is that the payment of the purchase price extends to all men (2 Pet. 2:1) but that the deliverance (Gal. 3:13) and release for service (1 Pet. 1:18, 19) are only for those who accept the payment.

Those who are determined to hold to a limited redemption at all costs find passages such as 2 Peter 2:1 most difficult to explain.

Calvin glosses over the problem in his discussion of this passage by simply emphasizing the necessity of the believer to live a life in accord with the high cost of redemption.[31] Owen attempts an explanation in a footnote to Calvin's treatment. He tries to remove the problem by removing the force of the word "bought." ". . . They denied Christ as their sovereign, as they rendered no obedience to him, though they may have professed to believe in him as a Saviour."[32]

The fact is the word which is here translated "bought" does not mean "sovereign." As we have before noted, it is one of the three great words in the New Testament often translated "redeem." And that is precisely what it means. Thayer indicates that the word means "to buy."[33] It cannot be avoided that Peter is here saying, in words unmistakably clear, Christ paid the ransom price even for those who deny Him.

Hodge makes a less serious attempt to answer the problem when he simply includes the reference along with others such as John 3:14-17, 1 John 2:2, 1 Timothy 2:3, 4 and says: "In all these and the like cases the words *all* and *all men* evidently mean Jew and Gentile."[34]

Some even argue that, since the name of Christ is not mentioned here but the word "Lord" or "master" is used instead,

---

[31] John Calvin, *Commentaries on the Catholic Epistles,* trans. and ed. John Owen (Grand Rapids: Wm. B. Eerdmans Publishing Co., 1948), p. 393.

[32] *Ibid.,* footnote No. 2.

[33] John Henry Thayer, *A Greek-English Lexicon of the New Testament* (New York: American Book Co., 1889), p. 8.

[34] Hodge, *op. cit.,* p. 426.

therefore this is a reference to God the Father.[35] Whatever difference this makes is difficult to understand. Of course, God the Father was involved in redemption since He "sent" the Son. About all Gill has to offer on the passage is not an exegesis of it but rather a rejection of the clear teaching of the words. Without any attempt to explain the meaning of the words, Gill simply says: "Besides, if such as Christ has bought with His blood should be left to so deny Him as to bring upon themselves eternal destruction, Christ's purchase would be in vain, the ransom-price paid would be for nought—which can never be true."[36] Gill has forgotten, evidently, that the text does say the Lord paid the purchase price whether it is believed or not. What the text does not say here or anywhere else is that the purchase price was paid for nought for those who reject it. That is an unwarranted conclusion drawn by those who refuse to allow Scripture to speak for itself.

At best these explanations of an obvious and clear teaching of Scripture only serve to reveal the futility of imposing restrictions where Scripture does not place them. Walvoord's conclusion to the study of the doctrine of redemption in the Bible is in keeping with the teaching of Scripture, even though it may conflict with the viewpoint of extreme Calvinists. "The study of redemption in Christ in the New Testament reveals a clear teaching that Christ by act of substitution in His death on the cross paid the ransom price and redeemed the enslaved *sinner* from his sinful position before God. Christ's death constituted an act of purchase in which the *sinner* is removed from his former bondage in sin by payment of the ransom price [italics mine]."[37]

Propitiation

Based on the direct usage of the idea of propitiation in both the Old and New Testaments, *propitiation* means to "satisfy," "appease" or "placate." When used in relation to the atoning work of Christ, this very same idea is conveyed (Rom.

---

[35] John Gill, *The Doctrine of Particular Redemption*, p. 29.
[36] *Ibid.*
[37] Walvoord, "Redemption," *Bibliotheca Sacra*, CXIX (January-March, 1962), p. 11.

3:25; Heb. 2:17; 1 John 2:2; 4:10). "Propitiation presupposes the wrath and displeasure of God, and the purpose of propitiation is the removal of this displeasure. Very simply stated, the doctrine of propitiation means that Christ propitiated the wrath of God and rendered God propitious to his people."[38]

This in no way implies that the love of God is restrained or held back because of propitiation. It is not a matter of either propitiation or love on the part of God but rather it is His infinite love which provided the propitiation or satisfaction of His person in Christ. Neither are we ever to understand that Christ's propitiatory sacrifice turned the wrath of God into love. That is, God must never be viewed as One Who became soft and easygoing and simply overlooked, because of some emotional stress, the true intensity of His hatred for sin. No! He poured out the full judgment of sin on Christ. He bore it all. "It is one thing to say that the wrathful God is made loving. That would be entirely false. It is another thing to say the wrathful God is loving. That is profoundly true. But it is also true that the wrath by which he is wrathful is propitiated through the cross."[39]

Pagan usage of the word *propitiation* relates it to the appeasing of a heathen god. "The uniform acceptation of the word in classical Greek, when applied to the Deity, is the means of appeasing God, or of averting His anger; and not a single instance to the contrary occurs in the whole Greek literature."[40] The necessity of appeasing a deity implies the wrath and anger of that offended deity.

It is readily agreed that Old Testament usage of the word *propitiation* in the Septuagint does not involve satisfying the crude and unreasonable deities of heathen culture. The Old Testament concept of a righteous but offended God Who is satisfied by a propitiation includes not only His wrath but also His everlasting love, and this makes the difference. Jehovah's

---

[38] John Murray, *Redemption—Accomplished and Applied* (Grand Rapids: Wm. B. Eerdmans Publishing Co., 1955), p. 36.

[39] *Ibid.*, pp. 37, 38.

[40] George Smeaton, *The Apostles' Doctrine of the Atonement* (Grand Rapids: Zondervan Publishing House, 1957), p. 455.

wrath in the Old Testament, as well as in the New Testament for that matter, is His holy reaction to sin (Job 21:20; Ezek. 16:38; Jer. 6:11; 2 Chron. 28:11-13; 2 Kings 13:3; Neh. 13:18). The difference between the concept of propitiation in pre-Biblical heathenism and in the Old Testament is not to be found in the fact or nature of it but rather in the character of the one who is propitiated. The God of the Bible is holy, just and righteous altogether and not vengeful as the heathen gods were represented to be. "The Bible writers have nothing to do with pagan conceptions of a capricious and vindictive deity, inflicting arbitrary punishments on offending worshippers, who must then bribe him back to a good mood by the appropriate offerings."[41]

Though pagan ideas of wrathful deities are foreign to the Scriptures this does not mean, as the modern Biblical critic asserts, that there is no concept of wrath and satisfaction found in the Bible. "In view of the abundant evidence in the Old Testament describing God as a deity who must bring judgment upon the sinner, a serious question may be raised as to whether the attempts of modern writers to eliminate the idea of the wrath of God entirely from the Old Testament is a justifiable procedure. It is more accurate to conclude that the doctrine of the righteousness of God is coupled with the love and mercy of God in the Old Testament. The harmony established between these attributes by the doctrine of satisfaction for sin is embodied in propitiation."[42]

We have been attempting to show that there is a difference in the concept of propitiation in the Old Testament from that in pre-Biblical paganism. That difference, it has been noted, lies in the fact that the God to be satisfied in the Old Testament is not only a God of wrath but also a God of love, righteousness and mercy. There is another difference which separates the Biblical concept of propitiation from that of heathenism. The God of the Scriptures not only demands total and complete satisfaction from the offender but also has in and through His in-

[41] Morris, *The Apostolic Preaching of the Cross,* p. 129.
[42] John F. Walvoord, "Propitiation," *Bibliotheca Sacra,* CXIX (April-June, 1962), p. 99.

finite love provided mankind with such a propitiation—His Son, Jesus Christ, the righteous One.

The most important text of Scripture dealing with propitiation and the extent of the atonement is given by John: "My little children, these things write I unto you, that ye sin not. And if any man sin, we have an advocate with the Father, Jesus Christ the righteous: And he is the *propitiation for our sins*: and not for ours only, but *also for the sins of the whole world* [italics mine]" (1 John 2:1, 2).

One finds it hard to imagine how John could have been any clearer in stating the universal aspect of the atonement than he was in this passage. The normal, unbiased approach to this text evidences the fact that the propitiation was not only "for our sins" but also "for the sins of the whole world." When it is remembered that propitiation in the Biblical context involves God's wrath and vicarious substitution, the extending of this to the "whole world" provides strong argument for an unlimited atonement.[43] The intensity of the argument here is not lessened by the fact that the last phrase of the verse ought to read "but also for the whole world" rather than "but also for the sins of the whole world." The words "the sins of" in this latter phrase were added by the translators for clarification.[44] The fact of the universal extent remains, however.

The fact that this book was written to Christians and that the writer is concerned in the immediate context with sinning Christians does not militate against the universality of the propitiation in verse 2. Writers of Scripture must be allowed to widen their messages beyond those Christians to whom they addressed themselves. This is done frequently in Scripture as the writers in the clearest language possible extend their meanings to others. Furthermore, the very context in 1 John is filled with contrasts between the saved and the unsaved, between

---

[43] We need not be concerned here with contemporary denials of substitution in propitiation. Usually these revolve around the unfounded and unbiblical idea that God's love makes substitution for sin unnecessary. Limited redemptionists agree that propitiation includes substitution and therefore our purpose will be to study the extent of that substitution in this text.

[44] This ellipsis is a very common occurrence according to the Greek scholar Alford, *op. cit.*, IV, p. 433.

the ones obeying God's commandments and walking in the light and the ones without the love of God in them, denying Jesus Christ.

Some limited redemptionists insist that propitiation in Scripture has nothing to do with the redemptive or atoning work of Christ's sacrifice for sin. They relate the work of Christ in propitiation to the work associated with the mercy seat of the Old Testament (Lev. 16:14). There is some justification for this since both in the Septuagint and in Hebrews 9:5 the word for propitiation is used for mercy seat. The mercy seat in the Old Testament was that place where the high priest came on the Day of Atonement and sprinkled the blood which had been shed on the altar. Thus, it is argued, Christ's death fulfilled the type, and His death was for His people only, just as the blood sprinkled on the mercy seat was for Israel only.

When the above argument is used to dissociate propitiation from Christ's substitutionary work in redemption, two weaknesses are evident. First of all, propitiation is related to redemption in Scripture. In 1 John 4:10 the same writer associates God's love with the giving of His Son ". . . to be the propitiation for our sins." Too, in Romans 3:24, 25, Paul very clearly connects redemption in Christ Jesus with "propitiation through faith in his blood." The scriptural usage of the word for propitiation and its cognates demonstrates that Christ was not only the place of propitiation (mercy seat) but also the very sacrifice itself. Secondly, it must be remembered, even if it be granted that the 1 John 2:2 reference refers back to the mercy seat in the Tabernacle, that the blood sprinkled there was for "the people" and surely not all those represented were of the number of the elect. For this attempt in associating propitiation with the mercy seat alone to be valid as an argument against the universality of the atonement one would need to assume that the high priest was only offering the sacrifice for elect Israelites. This is a most untenable position unless one is prepared to make every Jew thus being represented an elect or saved Jew. It is doubtful that anyone would wish to go to that extreme.

All attempts to restrict the extent of the atonement in this passage are futile. To make the first phrase, "for our sins," and the last phrase, "for the whole world," both refer to the elect reduces John's clear statement to a redundancy. If that be the case, John is saying the same thing twice. Notice how meaningless the passage becomes if the limited concept be applied: "And he is the propitiation for our sins [sins of the elect]: and not for ours only, but also for the whole world [world of the elect]." Neither is the difficulty alleviated when "our sins" is made to refer to the sins of elect Jews and "sins of the whole world" made to refer to sins of elect Gentiles.[45] John knew the words for "Jews" and "Gentiles" and could have used them had that been his intention. Paul did not hesitate to use those words when describing the universality of guilt (Rom. 3:9).

Pink does what most limited redemptionists do in dealing with the word "world" here. He arbitrarily limits it to the elect. Yet when the same word occurs in a text dealing with man's sin, he broadens its meaning. " 'Kosmos' is used of the whole race: Rom. 3:19, etc."[46]

Westcott's comment on the extent of the propitiation in this passage is helpful: "But for all alike Christ's propitiation is valid. The propitiation extends as far as the need of it (l.c.) through all place and all time. Comp. iv.14 (John iv.42; xii.32; xvii.22-24)."[47] A. T. Robertson's comment is equally appropriate: "At any rate, the propitiation by Christ provides for salvation for all (Heb. 2:9) if they will only be reconciled with God (II Cor. 5:19-21)."[48]

It is indeed interesting to note how those who believe in limited atonement deal with this clear passage. One such writer put it this way: "What, then, does he mean when he calls it a propitiation for the whole world? He intimates that it was not for him and for those to whom he wrote alone, but for the redeemed of every period, place, and people—that is, prospectively and retrospectively. The apostle connects the intercession and propitiation in such a way as to show that Christ's work is ap-

---

[45] Arthur W. Pink, *The Sovereignty of God* (Cleveland: Cleveland Bible Truth Depot, 1930), pp. 315-318.
[46] *Ibid.*, p. 312.
[47] B. F. Westcott, *The Epistles of St. John* (Grand Rapids: Wm. B. Eerdmans Publishing Co., 1952), p. 45.
[48] Robertson, *op. cit.*, VI, p. 210.

plicable to all the redeemed who then lived, or had ever lived, or should ever live, wherever found in the nations of the earth, and in whatever age. This is the point of the distinction; it is not the distinction elsewhere expressed between Jew and Gentile."[49]

This kind of explanation fits into the limited viewpoint very well, but whether it fits the Biblical meaning of the words involved is another matter entirely. One questions the right of the interpreter to make the word "world" mean the "redeemed." Such arbitrary and forced meanings will not tolerate the searchlight of an honest inquiry.

Murray admits that no text in Scripture presents more plausible support for the doctrine of universal atonement than this one (1 John 2:1, 2). "It must be said that the language John uses here would fit in perfectly with the doctrine of universal atonement if Scripture elsewhere demonstrated that to be the biblical doctrine."[50] After making this admission, Murray proceeds to argue that since other Scripture teaches a limited atonement, therefore, this one must be so interpreted also. He presents a threefold argument to explain John's universal statement. First, he says John is setting forth the "scope" of Jesus' propitiation; that is, it was not limited in its virtue and efficacy to the immediate disciples. Second, John desired to emphasize the "exclusiveness" of Jesus as a propitiation. No one else but Jesus could be the propitiation. Third, John needed to remind his readers of the "perpetuity" of Christ's propitiation. That is to say, the propitiation which Jesus made endures forever and never loses its efficacy.[51]

Murray has here performed an excellent service in describing the nature of the work of Christ in propitiation. The only problem is that John was not dealing with the nature of that work but with the *extent* of it. Murray has not dealt with the problem which his view of the atonement faces in this passage.

This explanation given by Murray seems to be the best the limited redemptionist can offer. Calvin refuses to discuss the

---

[49] Smeaton, *op. cit.*, p. 460.
[50] Murray, *op. cit.*, p. 82.
[51] *Ibid.*, p. 83.

problem and simply insists that ". . . the design of John was no other than to make this benefit common to the whole church."[52] Hodge's explanation is even less definitive because he groups the passage with the other references to "all" and "world" and evidently sees no special problem.[53]

John Owen, however, devotes much space to this verse. His view may be summarized best in his own words: ". . . That as by the world in other places, men living in the world are denoted, so by the whole world in this can nothing be understood, but men living throughout the whole world, in all the parts and regions thereof (in opposition to the inhabitants of any one nation, place, or country as such). . . ."[54]

This explanation by Dr. Owen should demonstrate that limited redemptionists simply will not allow writers of Scripture to mean "world" when they say "world," even when they generalize and particularize in the same passage. One looks in vain for contextual evidence for such limitations.

Reconciliation

This is basically a New Testament doctrine with little contribution coming from the Old Testament or the Septuagint. Even in the New Testament the specific word for reconciliation used in relation to the death of Christ occurs in only a few passages (i.e., Rom. 5:10ff; 2 Cor. 5:18-20; Col. 1:20ff). Of course, the concept of reconciliation pervades many portions of the New Testament even where the word does not occur. It is believed by some to be the basic idea of the atonement and the best New Testament word to describe the purpose of the atonement.[55]

The basic Greek word for reconciliation is *katallasso* and it means *"to change, exchange* (esp. of money); hence, of persons, *to change* from enmity to friendship, *to reconcile*."[56] On

---

[52] Calvin, *Commentaries on the Catholic Epistles*, p. 173.
[53] Hodge, *op. cit.*, p. 424.
[54] Owen, *op. cit.*, V, p. 440.
[55] Morris, *The Apostolic Preaching of the Cross*, p. 186 citing T. H. Hughes and Vincent Taylor.
[56] G. Abbott-Smith, *A Manual Greek Lexicon of the New Testament* (New York: Charles Scribner's Sons, 1956), p. 236.

the basis of this meaning, Johnson defines reconciliation in relation to the atonement as ". . . a finished work of God by which man is brought from an attitude and position of enmity with God to an attitude and position of amity and peace with God by means of the removal of the enmity through the cross. To be effective it must, of course, be received in faith (cf. Rom. 5:10; 2 Cor. 5:20)."[57]

Chafer concurs with this definition: "In the New Testament its meaning is that of a complete and thorough change accomplished by the actual removal of the cause of enmity, so making reconciliation."[58]

Among those who have studied the doctrine of reconciliation there has been little difference as to the meaning of the term in Biblical usage. However, there have been a number of views as to who is reconciled—God, man or both—even among evangelical theologians.[59] A great deal of this difference of opinion arises because of a confusion of terms. If the Biblical terms are employed with the meaning which they have in the Bible, the difficulty is lessened considerably. Those who speak of God as reconciled usually mean God's attitude is changed toward the sinner because of the death of Christ, but this is described in the Bible as propitiation, not reconciliation. The fact is that Scripture nowhere states that God is ever reconciled (changed). On the contrary, the abundant testimony of Scripture is that man is reconciled to God (Rom. 5:10; 2 Cor. 5:18).

No doubt it should be emphasized that the reconciling work of God is related in Scripture to the death of Christ and not to His incarnation. Contemporary liberal and neo-orthodox writers, in keeping with their denial of the vicarious and substitutionary

---

[57] S. Lewis Johnson, "From Enmity to Amity," *Bibliotheca Sacra*, CXIX (April-June, 1962), p. 144.

[58] Chafer, *Salvation*, p. 34.

[59] W. G. T. Shedd, *Dogmatic Theology*, II, pp. 395-397, holds that God is reconciled. Charles Hodge, *Systematic Theology*, II, p. 514, believes God and man are reconciled. A. H. Strong, *Systematic Theology*, p. 886, on the other hand, insists that man alone is reconciled. Likewise, Owen, *op. cit.*, V, pp. 356-359, Calvin's interpreter and champion of limited atonement, views reconciliation as related to God and man. He speaks especially of God being reconciled, and thus he cannot accept unlimited atonement because God's wrath rests upon some and this would mean God is not reconciled to all. Owen failed to recognize that Scripture never speaks of God as reconciled.

nature of Christ's death, place emphasis upon His incarnation
and life as God's means of displaying His love and thus reconciliation. No one would deny the necessity of the Incarnation to
the reconciling cross-work of Christ; yet according to Scripture
it was His death which brought about the reconciliation. In
the greatest passage on reconciliation as it relates to man, the
death of Christ is mentioned frequently (Rom. 5:6-10). No wonder it could be said that ". . . The greatest passage which says that
God was in Christ reconciling says in the same breath that it was
by Christ being made sin for us. The reconciliation is attached
to Christ's death, and to that as an expiation."[60]

The crucial passage on reconciliation, which relates to the
extent of the reconciling work of Christ, is found in 2 Corinthians 5:18-20: ". . . God, who hath *reconciled us* to himself by
Jesus Christ, . . . was in Christ, *reconciling the world* unto himself. . . ." Reconciliation as it is used here refers to the change
which God wrought in the world of men through the death of
His Son. The apostle here declares this reconciliation to extend
to the redeemed, "us," and to the mass of mankind, "the world."
The change or reconciliation of the apostle and the believers to
whom he wrote produces in the reconciled one a responsibility
in the ministry of reconciliation (v. 18). The basis for this
ministry of reconciliation rests in the fact that God has altered,
changed or reconciled the world in relation to Himself (v. 19)
and for that reason we are ambassadors for Christ, beseeching
men to be reconciled to God (v. 20).

This passage is very similar to Romans 5:10, 11: "For if,
when we were enemies, we were reconciled to God by the death
of his Son, much more, being reconciled, we shall be saved by his
life. And not only so, but we also joy in God through our
Lord Jesus Christ, by whom we have now received the reconciliation." (The Authorized Version, unfortunately, has "atonement" instead of "reconciliation.") It is obvious from both of
these passages that reconciliation must be personally received to
be effective. The reconciling work of Christ was done before
anyone would or could respond to it. In the Corinthians text

[60] P. T. Forsyth, *The Cruciality of the Cross* (New York: Hodder & Stough-
ton, n.d.), p. 68.

God is said to have "reconciled the world" and "reconciled us to himself by Jesus Christ"; and in the Romans passage "we were reconciled to God by the death of his Son" while we were enemies and that accomplished reconciliation must be "received" to be effective.

From the grammatical standpoint it is important to note the tenses used in 2 Corinthians 5:18, 19. When speaking of the believer's reconciliation Paul uses the aorist tense, which denotes an act that is finished (v. 18). On the other hand, when speaking of the reconciliation of the world he uses the present tense, indicating the continuous process (v. 19). Evidently the apostle was in this way stressing the fact of the believers' reconciliation as an accomplished thing, both objectively and subjectively, since they had received Christ and thus His reconciling work by faith (cf. Rom. 5:10). The case is much different, though, as far as unbelieving mankind in general is concerned. True, according to the aorist tense used in verses 14 and 15, Christ died for all in an objective sense; yet, Paul, by his use of the present participle in verse 19, *"reconciling* the world unto himself, *not imputing* their trespasses unto them," is highlighting the fact that while the reconciling took place historically, there is a sense in which it is ever going on as men believe and thus appropriate the objective historical reconciliation by means of faith. Further emphasis upon this twofold aspect of reconciliation is found when Paul speaks of the ministry of reconciliation as "given" to each believer (v. 18) and the word of reconciliation as "committed" to us (v. 19). In both of these cases, the aorist tense is used which stresses the past fact of reconciliation as the basis of the ambassador's message (v. 20). The reason we can preach the message of reconciliation to a lost world and in fact the very basis of that message is the final and all-inclusive work which Christ accomplished on the cross.

Lenski's summarization of these verses is the result of careful and accurate exegesis. "What does Paul say? That what God has finished for him and for his helpers (aorist *katallazantos*) he is still busy with (durative present participles) in regard to the world, namely the individuals in it; that in steadily working at this reconciling and not reckoning to men their transgressions

God employed Paul and his helpers in the ministry which he gave them with the word of reconciliation that he deposited with them. This work began when Christ died, when 'God was in Christ,' when he wrought the objective reconciliation 'through Christ' (v. 18). That objective reconciliation includes the whole world. But it must be brought to the world, to be made a personal possession by faith, a personal, individual reconciliation by means of the ministry of the reconciliation and the word of the reconciliation."[61]

Of course, the limited redemptionists must again impose restrictions or limitations upon the death of Christ for "all" in 2 Corinthians 5:14, 15 as they must on the reconciliation of the "world" in verse 19. John Gill, for example, who refers to his view as that of particular redemption, has this to say of verses 14 and 15: "Let it be observed that in the supposition, 'if one died for all,' the word 'men' is not used. It is not 'all men,' but simply 'all.' All whom? It may be supplied from other Scriptures, 'all His people' whom Christ came to save. . . ."[62]

This explanation completely ignores the plain and obvious fact of the contrast between the "us" and "we" of verse 14 and the "all" of verses 14 and 15. Also, it fails to account for the phrase "they which live" in verse 15. As to the omission of the word "men" in the text, this is a common practice in Greek, especially in a case such as this where the ones constrained by the love of Christ are most assuredly men.

John Owen interprets "world" in verse 19 as the world of the elect. To do so he says: "They who are called the *world,* verse 19, are termed 'us'; verse 18 . . . by the *world* here can be meant none but the elect believers."[63] Or again he says, "The *world* here then is only the world of blessed pardoned believers, who are made the righteousness of God in Christ."[64]

Steele and Thomas dismiss this passage very quickly by associating it with other verses containing similar words and saying Christ died for all without distinction but not for all without

[61] Lenski, *op. cit.,* p. 1045.
[62] Gill, *op. cit.,* p. 22.
[63] Owen, *op. cit.,* V, p. 451.
[64] *Ibid.,* p. 452.

exception.[65] Murray and Hodge do not even deal with the passage when seeking to answer the objection to their limited view.

Now, these explanations surely fit the strict Calvinistic view of the atonement; there is no doubt about that. There are doubts, though, that these attempts of arbitrary limitation fit the context and content of Scripture.

Another passage of Scripture which expands and confirms this twofold aspect of reconciliation is found in Colossians 1:20-22: "And, having made peace through the blood of his cross, by him to reconcile all things unto himself; by him, I say, whether they be things in earth, or things in heaven. And you, that were sometime alienated and enemies in your mind by wicked works, yet now hath he reconciled In the body of his flesh through death, to present you holy and unblameable and unreproveable in his sight."

It seems rather clear from these verses that there was a universal provision of reconciliation as well as an individual application of that reconciliation with both aspects finding their origin in the death of Christ. There is mention of the reconciliation of "all things" (v. 20) and the personal and individual reconciliation of the individual (v. 21). This individual reconciliation, it should be noted, is related to those who were "alienated and enemies" of God.

"It should be clear from this passage, as well as from the others, that the act of reconciliation in the death of Christ does not in itself affect reconciliation for the individual, but rather that it is provisional and makes possible the reconciliation of the individual. The natural state of the unsaved continues unchanged even after the death of Christ until such time that the reconciling work is made effective in him when he believes."[66]

A question may be raised as to the necessity of the reconciliation of the "things in earth, or things in heaven" (v. 20). The answer lies in the extent of the curse of sin brought on the universe by Adam's transgression and the race's participation in it. According to Romans 8:22, ". . . the whole creation

---

[65] Steele and Thomas, *op. cit.,* p. 46.
[66] Walvoord, "Reconciliation," *Bibliotheca Sacra,* CXX (January-March, 1963), p. 8.

groaneth and travaileth . . ." and is affected by the curse of God because of sin. Seemingly, the earth, which was created perfect by God, was brought down to the level of fallen man when man fell. That curse will be lifted one day when the Lord restores it to its original status in the kingdom reign.

The point which we have been trying to make in the study of these three great aspects of Christ's work on the cross—redemption, propitiation and reconciliation—has been well summarized by another: "The relationship of redemption, propitiation, and reconciliation, therefore, becomes clear. Christ by His death redeemed or paid the price for sin. This payment constituted a propitiation or satisfaction of God's righteousness. This freed the love of God to act in grace toward the sinner in reconciling the sinner to Himself on the basis that Christ has died in his place. The believer who comes into the position of being in Christ through faith and through the baptism of the Holy Spirit (1 Cor. 12:13) thus is reconciled to God because God sees him in Christ. The whole act of reconciliation, therefore, is an act of God, a free gift to man, provided for all men, effective to those who believe. Those once estranged in Adam are now reconciled in Christ."[67]

---

[67] *Ibid.*, p. 5.

No more let sins and sorrows grow,
Nor thorns infest the ground;
He comes to make His blessings flow
Far as the curse is found,
Far as the curse is found,
Far as, far as the curse is found.

—Isaac Watts

IV

PROBLEMS WITH AN UNLIMITED VIEW OF THE ATONEMENT

The language of the Bible, when taken at face value, teaches a sense in which the atonement is both limited and unlimited. There are difficulties which must be faced with each of these views. Therefore, it is necessary to analyze the problems and determine their magnitude. If the difficulties are of too great proportion, perhaps the view one holds is Biblically indefensible. Here are some of the major problems raised against the moderate Calvinistic unlimited view by strict Calvinists holding to a limited concept.

I. *The Death of Christ and the Nonelect*

The matter could be put another way just as easily. What relation do the nonelect have to the death of Christ? The adherents of the unlimited view believe all men were included in a provisionary sense in the death of Christ, yet they strongly maintain that only those who believe appropriate, and thus benefit from that death. Charles H. Spurgeon disagrees with this viewpoint and states the question under consideration thus: "If Christ has died for you, you can never be lost. God will not punish twice for one thing. If God punished Christ for your sins He will not punish you."[1]

The answer to the problem is twofold. *First,* the Bible does not teach that Christ's death saves apart from faith. The accomplishments of the cross must be appropriated by those who would be saved and until such a time as faith is exercised the elect are just as lost as the nonelect. *Second,* John 3:18 declares the relation of the Son to the sinner who does not believe: "He that believeth on him is not condemned: but he that believeth not is condemned already, because he hath not believed in the name of the only begotten Son of God." The nonelect, or those for whom Christ paid the ransom price who do not believe (2 Pet. 2:1), are condemned on the basis of the cross. They are not condemned because they are of the nonelect or because Christ did not die for them but rather because they believe not in Him. Therefore the cross becomes a basis of judgment for the nonelect and God is not defeated when men are lost for whom Christ died.

Seeking to answer the question of what effect the provisional reconciliation of the world has upon the unsaved who never accept it, Walvoord gives this reply: "The answer seems to be that the basis for his condemnation and judgment has been essentially changed. Apart from the death of Christ, a sinner would have been committed to his eternal punishment regardless of what he had done. Even if he had placed faith in God, he would still be in Adam, and there would be no provision of reconciliation or salvation for him. The provision having been made, however, the whole world is placed in an entirely different light. A person now proceeds to eternal punishment not because God has failed to provide, or because the love of God has been ineffective, but rather because he has rejected that which God has provided. This is set forth plainly in John 3:18: 'He that believeth on him is not judged: he that believeth not hath been judged already, because he hath not believed on

---

[1] Charles H. Spurgeon cited by Loraine Boettner, *The Reformed Doctrine of Predestination* (Philadelphia: Presbyterian and Reformed Publishing Co., 1965), p. 155.

the name of the only begotten Son of God.' The condemnation of the sinner now is not simply because he is a sinner, but because he has rejected God's provision to care for his sin. Though he is still judged according to his works, his eternal punishment has a new character of being that which he chose in rejecting the love and grace of God in Christ."[2]

If God purposed in His infinite, perfect wisdom to promote His own glory by sending His Son to die for some who, He knew, would never believe, what is that to man? It is no more difficult to accept this fact than it is to accept the existence of sin and human suffering as a means whereby the sovereign God of all the universe is bringing and will bring glory to Himself. God's ultimate purpose is no different in the elect from what it is in the nonelect. It is for His own glory that He hath foreordained *whatsoever* comes to pass.

II. *Christ's Death for Specific Groups*

The Bible does say Christ died for Paul (Gal. 2:20), for Israel (John 11:51), and for the church (Eph. 5:25). We have seen also that the redemptive work of Christ is limited in other passages. What does the believer in unlimited redemption do with these?

The answer to this problem is simple: the limited redemptionist accepts them and harmonizes them beautifully into his system. "To the unlimited redemptionist these Scriptures present not the slightest difficulty. He interprets these great passages precisely as does his opponent. He believes in the sovereign election of God and the one and only heavenly purpose to gather out a redeemed people for heaven's glory. However, the limited redemptionist is not able to deal with the unlimited redemption passages as easily."[3]

Previously, it was noted that many of the references where the atonement is referred to as affecting a specific group must be extended beyond the immediate reference. Even the believer

---

[2] John F. Walvoord, "Reconciliation," *Bibliotheca Sacra,* CXX (January-March, 1963), p. 11.

[3] Lewis Sperry Chafer, *Systematic Theology* (Dallas: Dallas Seminary Press, 1950), III, pp. 202, 203.

in limited atonement must broaden the subjects of the atonement in some instances. Thus, some of these passages which are used to argue for the limited extent of the atonement are not as limited as they appear to be on the surface. Citing one example will suffice: Christ's death for Israel does not mean He did not die for Gentiles.

III. *Universalism*

"Universal redemption means universal salvation."[4] Loraine Boettner is not alone in this charge. It is a very common one. And, if Christ's death secures and guarantees the salvation of all those for whom He died, the charge is a valid one. If, however, the cross-work of Christ is potential for all but actual only for those who believe, the charge is completely groundless. This criticism is usually made with reference to the Arminian brand of unlimited redemption which also involves sufficient grace to all to believe if they will. This charge cannot be leveled at unlimited redemption as held by moderate Calvinism since in that view the divine design of the atonement was to provide a basis for salvation for all and to secure it to those who believe. In other words, the unlimited view equals universalism only if the design of the atonement be that which is held by limited redemptionists. If the cross not only offers salvation but also saves those included in its scope, apart from any other instrumentality, then of course all those for whom He died must be saved. We have seen that the Bible does not teach this as the design of the atonement. No one has ever been, or will ever be, saved apart from personal faith in Christ as Savior. The personal application of the finished work has nothing to do with the completeness of the work. In fact, the accomplishments of Christ on the cross are complete and final even if no one had ever appropriated their benefits.

IV. *The Completed Work of Christ*

The limited redemptionists are all very quick to marshal a host of passages which speak of the work of Christ in redemp-

---

tion, propitiation and reconciliation as complete. And, there is no doubt that there are many such passages. The Bible in no uncertain terms teaches the completeness of the work of Christ. His entire work is finished, and there is no more for Him to do. This fact in no way rules out that other host of passages (which limited redemptionists seldom marshal) which teach the necessity of personal faith in that completed work.

The Scriptures also speak many times of all God's electing purposes as complete and apart from any of man's responsibilities. Are we therefore to take such passages, divorce them from other passages which stress the need for faith, and say election saves? Would it not be quite logical simply to move back one step further in the limited view and assign salvation to election? If the cross saves, why could it not be said that election saves since it is all of God, irrevocable and final?

Chafer said that Christ's finished work ". . . is *actual* in its availability, but *potential* in its application."[5] The substitutionary work of Christ is complete and at the same time conditional. It is conditional in that its accomplishments must be appropriated by faith. This is the universal testimony of the Bible. Nowhere does the Bible teach that men are lost because of their participation in Adam's guilt (which participation was real, Rom. 5:12), nor does it teach they are lost for want of inclusion in the atonement. The only scriptural reason which can be assigned why men are lost is because they reject the great work God accomplished through His Son at Calvary. The cross does not apply its own benefits; neither is it the only saving instrumentality. No elect person was saved at the time of Christ's dying. All men, including the elect, live some part of their lives in open rebellion to God, thus demonstrating that the finished accomplishments of Calvary must be applied by faith to each individual before any saving value comes to that individual. If the logic of the limited redemptionist be followed to its end, there would be no need of the manifold work of the Holy Spirit in bringing a sinner to the Savior. This has always been true of any sacrifice required of God in Scripture. The passover lamb was killed; the blood

---

[5] Chafer, *op. cit.*, p. 196.

was shed. But it was of no avail unless applied to the doorpost. It is so with the Lamb of God, Who takes away the sin of the world (John 1:29).

V. *Sovereign Election and Unlimited Atonement*

Is it inconsistent to believe in both? If the electing purpose of God culminates in the cross and if the cross saves by applying its own benefits, this question must be answered in the affirmative. If, however, on the other hand, the electing purpose of God is not complete until those elected are in Glory and if the cross *provides* a salvation dependent upon faith for its reception rather than *secures* that salvation apart from faith, then the question must be answered with an emphatic no.

Because Arminians believe Christ's death actually *obtained* or secured the salvation of all and because they reject election, they naturally see an inconsistency in believing in sovereign election while denying limited atonement. Miley put it this way: "Indeed, such a previous election and a universal atonement cannot stand together."[6]

Many Calvinists, on the other hand, also see a real contradiction in believing in unconditional election and unlimited atonement at the same time. It is felt that, insofar as the universal offer of the gospel is concerned, an acceptance of God's election of certain men only is tantamount to an acceptance of Christ's atonement for certain ones only. This issue will be dealt with subsequently in chapter five. However, it should be stated here in preview that the seeming inconsistency is greatly alleviated when it is understood that Scripture does not present man as lost because he was not among the elect but because he has not received God's remedy for his sin (John 1:12; 3:18).

Why is it so unthinkable that a sovereign God could choose from among the sinful race of men certain ones to be saved, procure their salvation at the cross and at the same time provide salvation for all the lost? If one believes in double predestination (the predetermining of some to salvation and some to dam-

[6] John Miley, *The Atonement in Christ* (New York: Phillips & Hunt, 1883), p. 303.

nation), as the strict Calvinist does, inconsistency would exist in the unlimited view. Hodge states the problem this way: "It is purely unthinkable that the same mind that sovereignly predestinated the elect to salvation and the rest of mankind to the punishment of their sins should, at the same time, make a great sacrifice for the sake of removing legal obstacles out of the way of those from whose path it is decreed other obstacles shall *not* be removed."[7]

There is one thing wrong with Hodge's observation and that is the Bible nowhere teaches the predestination of the lost to Hell. That is a human deduction, quite common among strict Calvinists, from the fact that God has predestinated some to salvation. God does not take the responsibility for men going to Hell. He did not predetermine that they should go there; He merely passed by them and left them in their lost estate for which they are responsible.

Unlimited redemptionists who believe in sovereign election do not believe the results and benefits from Christ's death are the same for the nonelect as for the elect. They believe the salvation of the elect was provided at the cross and secured at the moment of faith, and that Christ's provision of salvation for the nonelect serves as a basis of condemnation because they do not receive it.

The very fact that Scripture presents men as lost because they are not rightly related to Christ and not because they are nonelect removes the "inconsistency." God's purpose in the cross was not only to provide an absolute redemption for the elect and to apply that redemption at the moment of faith, but also to provide a conditional redemption for the nonelect which becomes the basis of God's dealings with them.

It is no more inconsistent to believe in sovereign election and unlimited atonement than it is to believe in sovereign election and human responsibility—two parallel and complementary truths. We do so because it is Biblical. We do not reject one or the other because it is "unthinkable" or because we cannot

---

[7] Archibald Alexander Hodge, *The Atonement* (Grand Rapids: Wm. B. Eerdmans Publishing Co., 1953), p. 414.

reconcile them. We are called upon to believe the Word—not to reconcile it with our finite minds. Whether we understand it or not, and even if we cannot reconcile it with other truths, the fact remains that God has chosen men in Christ before the foundation of the world (Eph. 1:4; 2 Tim. 1:9). This is the clear and unmistakable teaching of Scripture. God has not been pleased to tell us why He chose some; nor has He told us why, after He has chosen, men must still believe in order that the choice and election may become a reality to the individual thus chosen. The closest we can get to an understanding of the basis and reason for His actions in this regard is found in Ephesians 1:11: "In whom also we have obtained an inheritance, being predestinated according to the purpose of him who worketh all things after the counsel of his own will."

To summarize, the reason moderate Calvinists believe in the sovereign election of individuals by God and do not accept limited atonement is simply that they believe the Bible teaches the one and not the other.

VI. *The Sin of Unbelief*

In a refutation of Arminianism, John Owen put the question bluntly: "God imposed his wrath due unto, and Christ underwent the pains of hell for, either all the sins of all men, or all the sins of some men, or some sins of all men. If the last, some sins of all men, then have all men some sins to answer for, and so shall no man be saved. If the second, that is it which we affirm, that Christ in their stead and room suffered for all the sins of all the elect in the world. If the first, why, then are not all freed from the punishment of all their sins? You will say, 'Because of their unbelief; they will not believe.' But this unbelief, is it a sin or not? If not, why should they be punished for it? If it be, then Christ underwent the punishment due to it, or not. If so, then why must that hinder them more than their other sins for which he died from partaking of the fruit of his death? If he did not, then did he not die for all their sins."[8]

---

[8] John Owen, *The Works of John Owen,* ed. Thomas Cloutt (London: J. F. Dove, 1823), X, pp. 173 ff.

Owen seems here to present the case as an either-or proposition. Either Christ died for the sin of unbelief and all for whom He died are saved, or He did not and no one is saved. In answer to this argument, as it was stated in a previous chapter, the sin of unbelief is always associated with the completed work of Christ and thus assumes a specific quality and is treated in a particular way in Scripture. Owen's argument may be reversed and the problem stated this way: If Christ's death apart from any other considerations included the sin of unbelief, why does God ask men to believe since they would not be lost for not believing? A request from God for faith to apply the benefits of the cross becomes redundant. Why should God ask men to believe if that is not the sole condition of salvation? Or why does it matter whether they believe or not if their rejection and unbelief in Christ as Savior has been paid for? Why ask men to exercise faith for salvation if they are saved already by virtue of election and the atonement? Limited redemptionists not only remove the voluntariness from faith but they also make it an unnecessary routine, the refusal of which Christ atoned for and the exercise of which cannot be avoided. This argument of Owen's and all limited redemptionists only serves to prove what we have sought to establish earlier, namely, that limited redemptionists believe the death of Christ saves. Faith, in actuality, becomes a rather unnecessary thing, and salvation has no condition whatsoever.

The necessity of faith for salvation serves to demonstrate the provisional aspect of the atonement. The sin of unbelief is a problem for the limited redemptionist, for if his view be carried through consistently it would mean the elect would not even be born in sin and thus would not be subject to the wrath and condemnation of God before they believe, nor would they ever need to be forgiven and declared righteous before God since that has already been done at the cross. Looking at this problem from the standpoint of those for whom Christ did not die, it could be said that they would not be lost for rejecting Christ as Savior since, according to the limited view, Christ is not offered to them nor has He died for them; therefore, He could not be rejected by them.

"It is both reasonable and Scriptural to conclude that a

perfect substitution avails for those who are saved: that, in the case of the elect, it is delayed in its application until they believe and in the case of the nonelect, it is never applied at all."[9]

VII. *Christ's Intercession*

How does Christ's intercession relate to the extent of the atonement? Frequently, those who believe in limited atonement equate the extent of Christ's death with the extent of His present work in intercession. Owen writes: "So then it is evident that both these are acts of the same priestly office in Christ; and if he perform either of them for any, he must of necessity perform the other for them also: for he will not exercise any act of duty of his priestly function in their behalf, for whom he is not a priest. And for whom he is a priest, he must perform both, seeing he is faithful in the discharge of his function to the utmost, in the behalf of sinners for whom he undertakes. These two then, oblation and intercession, must in respect of their objects be of equal extent, and can by no means be separated."[10]

Those who believe in unlimited atonement agree wholeheartedly with Owen that the oblation or redemption of Christ and the intercession of Christ both have their source and foundation in the death of Christ. Without His death there could be no intercession just as there could be no redemption. Likewise, they agree that Christ is the One to whom both belong. Unlimited redemptionists do not agree, though, with the assumption that because they both reside in Christ and find their source in His death that thereby they are of equal extent.

The fallacy of Owen's argument is revealed in the fact that Scripture associates Christ's priestly intercessory ministry with believers and not with unbelievers. Until the elect believe they do not enjoy the benefits that accrue from Christ's work in intercession. The extent and benefit of intercession is to the believer only, while the atonement is extended to the entire world. The extent of the one is clearly to all while the other is not.

It is assumed by those who insist Christ died only for the elect that because He did not pray for the nonelect, He did not

---

[9] Chafer, *op. cit.*, p. 201.
[10] Owen, *op. cit.*, V, p. 259.

die for them. This assumption is not only unwarranted logically, but it is also unscriptural. Limited redemptionists assume Christ did not die for everyone because He did not pray for everyone; and then they argue backwards by saying that since He did not pray for all men, He did not die for all men.

John Gill is guilty of such faulty reasoning: "Now, such who have an interest in his prayers, are a special people, opposed to *the world,* and distinguished from them by the peculiar character of being *given* to Christ by the Father; and therefore those for whom he died, being the same persons, must be a special and peculiar people. *It follows then that Christ died not for every individual of mankind since he does not intercede for everyone* [italics mine]."[11]

How is it that limited redemptionists do not carry through their limitations of words and texts when they approach John 17. When our Lord says, "I pray not for the world" (v. 9), why does not "world" mean here what limited redemptionists say it means in John 3:16? Too, what of the other uses of the word "world" in this passage? If ever the elect were contrasted with the world it is here; yet elsewhere we are told "world" refers to the elect.

There is no doubt about it—the primary thrust of Christ's intercessory prayer in John 17 is directed to believers. It must be remembered, however, that when Christ said, "Neither pray I for these alone, but for them also which shall believe on me through their word," He was praying for millions who had not yet been born and thus had not yet been saved.

The answer to the question raised at the beginning of this section is, therefore, partially answered by Christ Himself in the very prayer which is used to teach the equal extent of His intercession with His sacrifice. Intercession does relate to believers (elect people), and only after the exercise of faith. The relation of the extent of the atonement to Christ's work in intercession is thus determined by the acceptance of Christ's substitutionary death by faith. The Bible does not equate the two in extent.

---

[11] John Gill, *The Cause of God and Truth* (Evansville: Sovereign Grace Book Club, n.d.), p. 100.

That is done by those persistent in believing in limited atonement. Christ's priestly ministry is no problem to the moderate Calvinist since the condition of faith which makes actual the other accomplishments of Calvary also makes the potential intercessory ministry an actual thing for the regenerate sinner.

Summary

Two things of importance stand out in our reply to the problems which limited redemptionists find in the unlimited view. The issue seems to revolve around the divine design or purpose of the atonement and the crucial importance and place of personal faith in relation to salvation. If it be acknowledged that God's design in the death of His Son was to provide redemption for all, conditioned upon the reception of it by individual faith, the problems vanish. This we believe to be the clear and consistent testimony of Scripture.

There's a wideness in God's mercy,
Like the wideness of the sea;
There's a kindness in His justice,
Which is more than liberty.

For the love of God is broader
Than the measure of man's mind;
And the heart of the Eternal
Is most wonderfully kind.

—Frederick W. Faber

V

PROBLEMS WITH A LIMITED VIEW OF THE ATONEMENT

The previous discussion has revealed some of the difficulties which must be faced in the acceptance of an unlimited view of the atonement. Solutions were suggested for these problems consistent with the whole of Scripture and its teaching of the atonement.

It will now be well to seek answers for some of the problems which exist for the limited view. Some of the thoughts to be expressed here have been anticipated earlier. But it will be well not only to list the problems but also to see ramifications of these and to seek answers from the limited redemptionists themselves.

I. *The Universal Passages*

The answers of limited redemptionists to this problem have been presented earlier and need not be repeated here. However, a summary statement may be helpful at this point: a limitation is placed upon every use of such words as "all," "whosoever" and "world" when used in salvation passages or passages related to the atonement. The limitation is a prescribed one—it is always to the elect that these words refer.

In the year 1823 a dialogue between one who believed in limited atonement and one who did not was published in the Utica Christian Repository. Aspasio represents the limited view and Paulinus the unlimited view. Aspasio has just enumerated the various usages for the word "world" in Scripture. Though the reply of Paulinus is lengthy, it will be quoted here since it answers so well the limited redemptionists in this regard.

"I am willing to grant, for the sake of giving your objection all possible force, that these words are used in the various senses you mention. Not, however, that I believe the word 'world' is ever used for God's people as distinguished from others. What, then, is the force of your objection? It is plainly this, that because these words are sometimes used in a limited sense, they may be so used in the texts I have quoted, and that you are at liberty to put this construction upon them if you please. But where will this principle lead us? Let us apply it to a few cases. The word *God* is sometimes used to signify a civil ruler; therefore, according to this principle of interpretation, it may be so understood in any given text. 'In the beginning God created the heavens and the earth,' may mean, In the beginning a civil ruler created the heavens and the earth. The word *everlasting* is sometimes used to signify a limited duration; therefore, it may be so understood in any given text; and, 'These shall go away into everlasting punishment,' may mean, These shall go away into a punishment of limited duration. And when the saints are promised everlasting life, it may mean a life of limited duration. And when Christ is styled the 'Mighty God, the Everlasting Father,' it may mean, the mighty civil ruler, the Father of a limited duration. The word *salvation* is sometimes used to signify deliverance from a temporal calamity; therefore, it may be so understood in any given text, and there may be no salvation but deliverance from temporal calamities. The word *resurrection* is sometimes used to signify regeneration; therefore it may be so understood in any given text, and there may be no resurrection foretold in the Scripture but regeneration. The word *baptism* is sometimes used to signify sufferings; therefore, it may be so understood in any given text; and the command to the apostles to go and baptize all nations may mean that they should go and inflict sufferings upon all nations. A principle of interpretation which leads into such absurdities cannot be admitted as a correct rule of interpreting the Word of God. Under the operation of such a rule, the Bible would become, as some pretend it is, a book by which anything can be supported and nothing proved. Every part of it would become 'vague and ambiguous in its meaning.' "[1]

Rather than allowing each individual context to determine the meaning of universal terms such as "all," "world," "whosoever," "every man," etc., strict Calvinists approach the Bible with a theological conviction which restricts every single occurrence of universal terms in a salvation context. No explanation is given why the same words are understood in a restricted sense in salvation passages and not in others. Why does not "world" mean "world of the elect" when it is used in relation to Satan's ministry (John 12:31; 14:30)? Or in Christ's high priestly prayer (John 17), a prayer which some insist teaches limited atonement, how is it that "world" no longer means "world of the elect"? Seemingly, the only explanation to be given for these arbitrary and inconsistent meanings is to be found in the strict Calvinistic insistence that Christ did not die for all men. Being convinced of that, the limited redemptionist proceeds to defend his position by narrowing the meaning of words wherever the normal and literal meaning would contradict his premise.

II. *Natural Benefits from the Cross*

It seems somewhat contradictory to admit, as limited redemptionists do, ". . . that important natural benefits accrue to the whole human race from the death of Christ, and that in these benefits the unbelieving, the impenitent, and the reprobate also share,"[2] and at the same time to deny that Christ's substitution provided the basis of salvation for the nonelect. Why are some benefits extended to all men and others only to the elect?

---

[1] Jonathan Edwards and others, *The Atonement* (Boston: Congregational Board of Publication, 1859), p. 581.
[2] Louis Berkhof, *Systematic Theology* (Grand Rapids: Wm. B. Eerdmans Publishing Co., 1941), p. 438.

Where in the Word of God are the benefits of Christ's death divided into natural and spiritual in such a way that the non-elect involuntarily share in the one and are not allowed to benefit voluntarily from the other? Hodge stated the limited view this way: "Christ did literally and absolutely die for all men in the sense of securing for all a lengthened respite and many temporal benefits, moral as well as physical."[3]

Attempting to clarify the question of the extent of the atonement, another limited redemptionist put it this way: "The question is not whether many benefits short of justification and salvation accrue to men from the death of Christ. The unbelieving and reprobate in this world enjoy numerous benefits that flow from the fact that Christ died and rose again."[4]

Since the same death provided both temporal and spiritual benefits, how can it be said that the nonelect share in the temporal but have no relationship whatsoever to the spiritual? Does not the definite relationship between common grace[5] and the atonement link the nonelect to Christ's death? The very admission of limited redemptionists that some benefits extend to the nonelect means they make the design of God twofold, applying some benefits directly to the elect and others indirectly to the nonelect. Thus, there is inconsistency in the limited view when some of Calvary's achievements are made to extend to all men while others are restricted to the elect. Consistency would restrict all the benefits to the ones for whom Christ died; and since in the limited concept Christ died only for the elect, it is illogical to include the nonelect in any sense. If they are included at all, they must be included in it all since it was one sacrifice in which all the effects are grounded. Also, the Bible nowhere makes the distinction which strict Calvinists insist upon.

---

[3] A. A. Hodge, *The Atonement* (Grand Rapids: Wm. B. Eerdmans Publishing Co., 1953), p. 427.
[4] John Murray, *Redemption—Accomplished and Applied* (Grand Rapids: Wm. B. Eerdmans Publishing Co., 1955), p. 71.
[5] Common grace may be defined as the work of God in behalf of all men in His general care for them. It is to be contrasted with efficacious grace which always eventuates in salvation.

III. *The Love of God*

The Bible pictures love as part of the very nature of God. He must not strive to love! He is love (1 John 4:8). Limited redemptionists must not only restrict and limit the universal phrases such as "all" and "world"; they must also do the same with the word "love" since it frequently occurs with those words (i.e., John 3:16).

The problem is in no way lessened by assigning kinds of love to God (a certain kind to the nonelect and another kind to the elect) as Hodge does.[6] Nor is it solved by saying, ". . . Scripture does not teach . . . that God loves all men equally."[7]

Moderate Calvinists agree that the believer is the special object of God's love. They understand the "much more" abundance of the Father's care and concern for His own. This, however, is not the issue. The crux of the matter is, "Does God love all men or does He not?" God's love for the entire world not only is the clear teaching of the New Testament (i.e., John 3:16) but is also the emphatic revelation of the Old Testament. When explaining the choice of the Israelites as a nation, in which there were many rebels, God said, "The LORD did not set his love upon you, nor choose you, because ye were more in number than any people; for ye were the fewest of all people: But because the LORD loved you, and because he would keep the oath which he had sworn unto your fathers . . ." (Deut. 7:7, 8). Again, in a context dealing with idolatry and apostasy on the part of the nation, God reminded, "When Israel was a child, then I loved him, and called my son out of Egypt" (Hosea 11:1). Surely the love of God here expressed to the entire nation can in no sense be restricted to the elect of the nation, for God was not addressing the believing Israelites only but the whole nation in both instances, and He stated clearly that He loved all of them.

Even though some limited redemptionists do not like to hear other Calvinists say, ". . . God is good and benevolent to

---

[6] Hodge, *op. cit.*, pp. 382, 383.
[7] R. B. Kuiper, *For Whom Did Christ Die?* (Grand Rapids: Wm. B. Eerdmans Publishing Co., 1959), p. 68.

all the children of men but . . . He loves only the elect,"[8] the fact still remains that this is the only conclusion one can come to who believes in limited atonement. If all the references to love in the redemption passages refer to the elect, obviously God did not have the same love for the nonelect. Kuiper admits this to be the teaching of Scripture very candidly: ". . . It tells us that His love for the elect differs qualitatively from His love for others."[9]

An even more dogmatic observation comes from one determined to hold to limited atonement. "To tell the Christ-rejector that God loves him is to cauterise his conscience, as well as to afford him a sense of security in his sins. The fact is that the love of God is a truth for the saints only, and to present it to the enemies of God is to take the children's bread and cast it to the dogs."[10] Pink proceeds to defend this ridiculous statement by quoting dozens of verses of Scripture which speak of the wrath of God upon sinners. Of course God hates sin and will pour out His divine wrath upon sinners who reject His Son, and the unlimited redemptionist does not deny that. The fact is it is just such darkened, doomed, ungodly enemies and sinners upon whom God showers His grace (Rom. 5:8-10). The fact that God despises sin and will eternally punish sinners does not mean He does not love them. He demonstrated His eternal love at Calvary for Adam's race on whom the wrath of God was abiding. Nothing could be farther from the truth than to say God does not love sinners unless it would be to say He loves only a certain kind of sinner—an elect one. The testimony of Scripture is so abundantly opposed to such a fanciful and absurd view that to cite passages to the contrary would border on the ridiculous.

This attempt to assign limits arbitrarily to the degree and extent of God's love is without basis in Scripture. One wonders whether this might not also be done to the other divine attributes. Would limited redemptionists want to restrict any or all of the

---

[8] *Ibid.*
[9] *Ibid.*
[10] Arthur W. Pink, *The Sovereignty of God* (Cleveland: Cleveland Bible Truth Depot, 1930), p. 246.

other perfections of God to the elect only? If not, why not? There is not a thread of evidence which would lead one to confine any of the other attributes to just one segment of the human race. For example, who could ever conceive of God's exercising His holiness, righteousness, justice, omnipotence, omniscience and omnipresence in relation only to the elect? Why then may His complete and perfect love be so restricted? The fact is, it may not be restricted; at least it may not on scriptural grounds. To some strict Calvinists the fact that Scripture does not support their view does not seem to matter so long as Calvinists have held it in the past. Pink, for example, writes: "That God loves everybody is, we may say, quite a *modern* belief. The writings of the church-fathers, the Reformers or the Puritans will (we believe) be searched in vain for any such concept."[11] This observation is very general and may or may not be true, but it is not patent to the issue.

An attribute of God is not merely a characteristic of God which simply is attached to His person. God's attributes—all of them—are perfections of His being. They are part of His very nature. Therefore, those who would thus confine the love of God to the elect are guilty not only of arbitrarily restricting God's love, but also of placing limitations upon the very nature of God. Just because man cannot fathom how God could love His enemies and those whom He knew would never receive His Son is no reason for saying God's love is a truth for saints only. If God must wait until men are saints before He can love them, nobody would be loved by God until he is saved simply because nobody is a saint until that time.

Viewing the attempt of limited redemptionists from these scriptural perspectives makes their arguments appear very absurd and farfetched. The uniform testimony of Scripture is diametrically opposed to such restrictions of the love of our sovereign God. According to the Bible, Christ came to reveal the Father in all of His fulness to the entire world. "No man hath seen God at any time; the only begotten Son, which is in the bosom of the Father, he hath declared him" (John 1:18). Christ is here

---

[11] *Ibid.*

seen as the great and final Revealer of the Father to men. The Son exposed the Father to the world. And He made Him known fully and to the entire world, not just to the elect. He was the "true Light, which lighteth every man that cometh into the world" (John 1:9), the Revealer of God to all men (John 1:18) and the "Lamb of God, which taketh away the sin of the world" (John 1:29).

It seems that limited redemptionists are determined, at any cost, to force Scripture into their mold. This is done by them with regard to the love of God by taking for granted that which they seek to prove. They begin by arguing that it was a special love to the elect which induced Christ to die. But what of this premise? Granted that the death of Christ was a revelation and demonstration of the greatest love ever shown; yet, does this prove it was only for the elect?

IV. *The Universal Offer of the Gospel*

William Cunningham labels the scriptural command to preach the gospel to all "by far the most important and plausible of the scriptural arguments in support . . ."[12] of unlimited atonement. He admits that some Calvinists such as John Gill denied that the Scriptures taught a universal offer of the gospel. For our part, Gill and others, such as some of the English Baptists, carried the limited atonement view to its logical conclusion. If Christ died only for the elect, then why take that message to the nonelect? An even more sobering question would be, "Why does God invite all men if Christ did not provide for all?" It is *His* invitation which is universal and man merely takes it to men.

Dr. James Richards, a Calvinist who rejected limited atonement, stated the problem clearly: "We argue it from the indefinite tender of salvation made to all men where the Gospel comes. To us, no maxim appears more certain *than that a salvation offered implies a salvation provided*; for God will not

---

[12] William Cunningham, *Historical Theology* (Swengel, Pennsylvania: Bible Truth Depot, 1960), II, p. 344.

tantalize his creatures by tendering them with that which is not in his hand to bestow."[13]

Limited redemptionists recognize this inconsistency in their view. Thomas J. Crawford, who is considered an outstanding adherent to the limited view and who is thought to have produced one of the greatest works in its defense, said: "That there is great difficulty in the way of harmonizing the general invitations of the Gospel on the one hand with the special reference of the atonement to those who shall eventually be partakers of its benefits on the other hand—it would be altogether fruitless to disguise."[14]

Crawford attempts to solve the problem by saying that these two things—limited redemption and the universal offer of the gospel—are not within man's ability to reconcile. This he says is true because the one (he does not say which one) exceeds the power of our faculties to understand it. He then proceeds to offer some suggestions to avert the difficulty. *First,* there is some benefit in the cross for all and the gospel invitation conveys nothing more than this. *Second,* the same Scripture which invites all to salvation also has a special reference to the elect. *Third,* the command of God to preach the universal gospel is an expression of His desire and delight but is not declarative of His fixed purpose and determination. *Fourth,* the limited view is in no more difficulty than the Arminian view since some are lost to whom the message is preached.[15]

Hodge also admits the problem. "There is unquestionably a difficulty in the neighborhood, but it will require some discrimination to determine exactly the point upon which the difficulty presses."[16] His attempt fails to satisfy the demands of Scripture, however. He acknowledges that even though it could be demonstrated that the atonement was universal, our right to offer it to all does not rest upon that but upon the Great Commission. Hodge, too, finds refuge in the sovereignty of God

---

[13] James Richards, *Lectures on Mental Philosophy and Theology* (New York: N. W. Dodd, 1846), p. 322.
[14] Thomas J. Crawford, *The Doctrine of Holy Scripture Respecting the Atonement* (Grand Rapids: Baker Book House, 1954), p. 510.
[15] *Ibid.,* pp. 510-513.
[16] Hodge, *op. cit.,* p. 418.

for his answer. He insists that it is man's duty to repent and believe whether he can, or will, or not. Hodge's final attempt to reconcile the problem is his observation that those who believe in election and who reject limited atonement have the same problem as those who believe in limited atonement.[17]

This final attempt of Hodge to alleviate the limited redemptionist's difficulty by assigning the same difficulty to unlimited redemptionists is not valid. First, it is not valid as an answer to the problem because it is merely an attempt to avoid the contradiction by finding others with a similar problem. It sounds like the "misery-loves-company" idea. Second, it is not valid since the unlimited redemptionist simply does not have the problem Hodge assigns to him. The proclamation of the universal message of the gospel which includes an unlimited view of the atonement is entirely separate from God's electing purposes. Election is God's business, and we are not told to preach election to all men; we are told to preach Christ and Him crucified to everyone. Therefore, the moderate Calvinist can sincerely believe in sovereign election, obey the divine injunction, and yet preach that Christ died for all men without any inconsistency whatsoever either in his own mind or in his message. The command to preach the gospel to all men is always associated with Christ's death for all and not with God's election of some.

Kuiper follows suit in acknowledging the seriousness of this problem with limited redemption: "It cannot be denied that the Calvinist here faces a paradox. Significantly, he has no interest in denying the paradox, if only the term *paradox* be given its proper content."[18] Kuiper also resorts to the sovereignty of God and admits that since both the particular design of the atonement and the universal offer of the gospel are taught in Scripture, all man can do is find refuge in Romans 11:33. The final appeal which Kuiper makes centers in the content of the gospel or good news which we are to proclaim. Says Kuiper, we must tell men that Christ died for the ungodly (Rom. 5:6), that God makes a *bona fide* offer to men and that He will not re-

---

[17] *Ibid.*, pp. 418-423.
[18] Kuiper, *op. cit.*, p. 86.

fuse any who come to Him.[19] In other words, according to this
point of view, the gospel is not to be personalized but presented
in more general terms. And this is precisely the way it must
be in the strict Calvinistic approach. The only ones who can
ever be really sure that Christ died for them are the believers.
This, of course, runs counter to the New Testament emphasis
upon the command to take the gospel, which has at its very heart
the death of Christ, to all men; and it also removes the personal element which is necessary for salvation. Where is there
room for any stress upon the individual's lost condition and hope
of salvation in Christ if one is never sure that Christ died for
each and every person? Beyond dispute, the Bible makes the responsibility to carry the message of the gospel and to receive
it an individual matter.

It must be admitted that these are honest efforts to solve
a very perplexing problem faced by the limited redemption view.
It must also be acknowledged that the attempts have not in any
way lessened the difficulty. The one who believes in sovereign
election and an unlimited atonement has no problem as a believer and as a proclaimer of the universal and sovereign offer
of God's saving grace. Neither does he have a problem in personalizing the need of each man to accept that grace. He knows
the nonelect will not be saved, and he knows that the elect will
be in God's time. The difficulty which the limited redemptionist
faces is removed for the one who believes in unlimited redemption
because he is free to announce that Christ actually did die
for all men, quite to the contrary if one knows that some to whom
he speaks are without any provision whatsoever and have no
part in the sufficiency of Christ's death. ". . . It is no longer
a question in his mind of whether they will accept or reject;
it becomes rather a question of *truthfulness* in the declaration
of the message."[20]

W. Lindsay Alexander stated the issue clearly regarding the
point under discussion: "On this supposition the general invitations and promises of the gospel are without an adequate basis,

---

[19] *Ibid.*, p. 94.
[20] Lewis Sperry Chafer, *Systematic Theology* (Dallas: Dallas Seminary Press,
1950), III, p. 195.

and seem like a mere mockery, an offer, in short, of what has not been provided. It will not do to say, in reply to this, that as these invitations are actually given we are entitled on the authority of God's word to urge them and justified in accepting them; for this is mere evasion."[21]

A question might be introduced at this point. "Why is the universal gospel message incumbent upon the children of God?" According to 2 Corinthians 5:18, 19, it is not because of election or even because of a supposed covenant of redemption but solely because of the universal reconciliation which God wrought in Christ at the cross. Never is the ambassador of Christ told to inform people of their election in Christ or lack of it. Rather he is told to announce the good news that Christ died, was buried and arose again for sinners.

The discussion of this inconsistency in the limited view may best be concluded with Chafer's piercing remark: "To say, at one time, that Christ did not die for the nonelect and, at another time, that His death is the ground on which salvation is offered to all men, is perilously near contradiction."[22]

V. *The Covenant of Grace*

Berkhof, a limited redemptionist and a covenant theologian, defines the covenant of grace as ". . . that gracious agreement between the offended God and the offending but elect sinner, in which God promises salvation through faith in Christ, and the sinner accepts this believingly, promising a life of faith and obedience."[23] Reformed theologians argue for at least two covenants—the one described above and also a covenant of works which existed between God and Adam, promising him life for obedience and death for disobedience, which, incidentally, would result in salvation by works. The covenant of grace was necessitated because of the failure of the covenant of works. Some other reformed theologians argue for still another covenant which they designate as the covenant of redemption. This was made,

---

[21] *Ibid.*, citing W. Lindsay Alexander, *A System of Biblical Theology*, II, p. 111.
[22] Chafer, *op. cit.*, p. 194.
[23] Berkhof, *op. cit.*, p. 277.

they say, between the Father and the Son in eternity past and deals with the relation of each to the plan of redemption. The covenant of redemption)ecomes the foundation of the covenant of grace for those who ι ccept it.

For our present purposes we are concerned only with the covenant of grace and the relation of limited redemption to it. It is no secret that among those who adhere to reformed and covenant theology (these are almost without exception limited redemptionists) the unifying purpose of Scripture is the salvation of the elect; and this is based upon the covenant of grace, which covenant God is supposedly to have made with the elect guaranteeing their salvation.[24] Thus one can easily see why covenant theologians are usually adherents of limited redemption. They would be very inconsistent in their overall theological viewpoint if they were not. Contrariwise, it seems equally as inconsistent for one who does not have the covenant of grace as the unifying purpose of Scripture, but adheres to a dispensational scheme of theology, to believe in limited atonement.

That the covenant of grace is basic to the limited view can be easily demonstrated. John Owen's first two arguments against the universality of the atonement are based on his understanding of the covenant. Of this covenant and its relation to the atonement he says: "Neither can any effects thereof be extended beyond the compass of this covenant; but now this covenant was not made universally with all, but particularly only with some, and therefore those alone were intended in the benefits of the death of Christ."[25] The one who subscribes to this covenant of grace and makes it the *modus operandi* of all God's work will naturally believe in limited atonement by directing all of God's work at the cross to the elect with whom He made the covenant and by which He brings it to fulfillment.

Because he accepted the covenant of redemption as essentially equivalent to the covenant of grace, A. A. Hodge speaks thus

---

[24] For a full discussion of the rise, validity and objections to covenant theology see John F. Walvoord, *The Millennial Kingdom* (Findlay, Ohio: Dunham Publishing Company, 1959), pp. 89-91; and Charles C. Ryrie, *Dispensationalism Today* (Chicago: Moody Press, 1965), pp. 177-191.

[25] John Owen, *The Works of John Owen,* ed. Thomas Cloutt (London: J. C. Dove, 1823), V, p. 325.

of its relation to limited redemption: "Christ died in execution of the terms of an eternal Covenant of Redemption formed between the Father and the Son. . . . If he died in pursuance of a mutual understanding between himself and the Father, if he shall see of the travail of his soul and be satisfied, and if every one that the Father gave him in that covenant shall be saved, then surely those who are not saved are not those for whom he died."[26]

Hear the words of another limited redemptionist as he relates the covenant idea to limited atonement: "The particularistic view of the design of the atonement harmonizes perfectly with the Scriptural teaching of the covenant of redemption. From eternity the persons of the Holy Trinity planned the salvation of a multitude whom no man can number. An essential element in that plan was the giving by the Father to the Son of all who ultimately would be saved."[27]

Crawford is equally as clear in his discussion: ". . . The Son of God received a certain *charge* or *commission* from His Father which He solemnly engaged and undertook to execute; and further, that the end contemplated in this arrangement was not merely the announcement of spiritual blessings but the *attainment* of them, in behalf of all such as should eventually believe in Christ."[28]

John Gill also associates the covenant-of-grace idea with limited atonement and does so to such a degree that he virtually rules out total depravity. Speaking of the ones involved in the covenant and thus the ones for whom Christ is said to have died he said, "The objects of redemption are the sons of God. . . . Now these sons, or children of God, are a peculiar number of men. They are those who are given to Christ by God, for Him to redeem. They are the seed promised to Him in the covenant, that He should see and enjoy, and to whom He stands in the relation of the everlasting Father. These are those on whose account He became incarnate, took 'part of the same flesh and blood.' And these are the many sons whom He brings

[26] Hodge, *op. cit.*, pp. 404-408.
[27] Kuiper, *op. cit.*, p. 65.
[28] Crawford, *op. cit.*, p. 148.

to glory (Heb. 2:10, 13, 14). Now these are not all men (that is, every man), they are not 'the children of the flesh' or such as are never born again for they are not the children of God."[29]

If this be the case, how is it that elect people can be born in sin? Since the "sons of God" are the people of the covenant for whom Christ died, He must have died for sons, not for sinners. Furthermore, why did He need to die if the members of the covenant were already His sons?

Without producing any further evidence for this necessary relation between the covenant of grace and limited atonement, it will be concluded that such a vital link does exist. The covenant of grace is not merely an auxiliary of limited atonement; it is an integral part of it. Therefore, in reply to our original inquiry, we must answer that the limited view of the atonement is based squarely on the idea of the covenant of grace and has no real theological basis without it.

The question is, "How scriptural is this covenant-of-grace idea?" It must be admitted immediately that none of the covenants of the covenant system are stated as such in Scripture. While this in itself does not make them antibiblical, it ought to make one cautious about developing an entire system of theology upon them as covenant theology does.

When one rejects the covenant-of-grace idea as it is presented by covenant theologians, it does not follow that he questions whether or not God will save the elect. There can be no doubt in this regard. God will bring His purposes to fruition. The question is, "Did the Father and the Son make in eternity past such a covenant with each other and with the elect which limited the redemptive work of Christ to the elect only?"

Covenant theologians labor long and hard to gather scriptural support for such a covenant. The simple fact is there is no Scripture which states the covenant of grace concisely. Evidence is usually presented from Genesis 3:15[30] or from the idea that God always acts on a plan or from passages such as Isaiah

---

[29] John Gill, *The Doctrine of Particular Redemption*, p. 9.
[30] Oswald T. Allis, "The Covenant of Works," *Basic Christian Doctrines*, ed. Carl F. H. Henry (New York: Holt, Rinehart, and Winston, 1962), p. 97.

53:6, 7; John 10:15, 17; Luke 22:29.[31] These passages simply do not state the covenant of grace or its supposed conditions. The entire covenant system is a deduction and not an induction from Scripture. Even if such an agreement between God and the elect did exist, whether explicitly stated in Scripture or not, it would not follow that this would become the one and only purpose of God in Christ. God must be allowed to exercise His sovereignty in many ways to bring glory to Himself. Covenant theology tends to put God in a soteriological straightjacket by restricting Him to the redemptive program as the only and all-inclusive means of bringing glory to Himself. In so doing, there is a rejection of the varying rules of life and economies under which man lived and God progressively revealed Himself and His will.

It is not our intention here to engage in an extended refutation of covenant theology. Suffice it to say that the most serious weakness of the system is the way in which the Biblical and unconditional covenants (i.e., Abrahamic, Gen. 12; Palestinian, Deut. 28—30; Davidic, 2 Sam. 7; New, Jer. 31—33) are subjected to the covenant of grace and thus stripped of their literalness and real significance for the people with whom they were made.[32]

The system of covenant theology is not to be found in the historic creeds of the church, nor was it proclaimed until after the Reformation. The Scriptures are simply forced into the covenant

---

[31] Hodge, *op. cit.*, pp. 406, 407.

[32] Those who adhere to the covenant system quite frequently accuse dispensationalists, who reject their system, of teaching several ways of salvation. This is simply not true of normative dispensationalism. Charles C. Ryrie has succinctly stated the dispensationalist's viewpoint concerning the way of salvation: "The dispensationalists' answer to the problem is this: The *basis* of salvation in every age is the death of Christ; the *requirement* for salvation in every age is faith; the *object* of faith in every age is God; the *content* of faith changes in the various dispensations. It is this last point, of course, which distinguishes dispensationalism from covenant theology, but it is not a point to which the charge of teaching two ways of salvation can be attached. It simply recognizes the obvious fact of progressive revelation. When Adam looked upon the coats of skins with which God had clothed him and his wife, he did not see what the believer today sees looking back on the cross of Calvary. And neither did other Old Testament saints see what we can see today. There have to be two sides to this matter—that which God sees from His side and that which man sees from his" (Ryrie, *op. cit.*, pp. 123, 124).

mold by its adherents. If the idea that God made a covenant before the foundations of the world promising to send His Son to die for the elect only is not clearly taught in Scripture, then it is altogether possible that its necessary concomitant—limited atonement—is not taught there either.

VI. *Christ's Active and Passive Obedience*

Can it be said that Christ died only for the elect and at the same time that He vicariously atoned for sin in His life and in His death? If this be true, and most limited redemptionists say it is, a serious difficulty arises.

By active obedience is meant those sufferings which pertain to Christ's ministry while on the earth. By passive obedience is meant those sufferings which pertain to Christ's ministry while on the cross. Murray explains it this way: "The real use and purpose of the formula is to emphasize the two distinct aspects of our Lord's vicarious obedience. . . . Christ's obedience was vicarious in the bearing of the full judgment of God upon sin, *and it was vicarious in the full discharge of the demands of righteousness* [italics mine]."[33] Hodge's explanation of the active obedience or life sufferings of Christ will help us. "He lived his whole life, from his birth to his death, as our representative, obeying and suffering in our stead and for our sakes; and during this whole course all his suffering was obedience and all his obedience was suffering."[34]

Whether or not Christ's life sufferings were atoning in the sense that His death sufferings were is highly debatable if not antiscriptural. Since a brief refutation of the substitutionary nature of Christ's life was presented earlier, our purpose here will be to present what seems to be an obvious contradiction as this relates to the atonement. If Christ's ministry prior to the cross is placed on the same level as His ministry on the cross, there is an evident discrepancy. Surely no one would deny that during His life the Savior ministered to more than the elect. The Scripture indicates that He ministered to many who

---

[33] Murray, *op. cit.*, pp. 27, 28.
[34] Hodge, *op. cit.*, p. 250.

never believed on Him. If He was man's representative, obeying and suffering in our stead all through His life, how and in what sense can this aspect of His ministry be said to be limited? And if it be argued that His life sufferings are to be kept distinct from His death sufferings, then what happens to the entire argument for the validity of an active and a passive obedience, and on what basis is such a distinction made? Berkhof, an able exponent of the covenant system and of the vicarious nature of Christ's life, stated the relationship between the active and passive obedience very clearly: "It is customary to distinguish between the active and passive obedience of Christ. But in discriminating between the two, it should be distinctly understood that *they cannot be separated.* The two accompany each other at every point in the Saviour's life. There is a constant interpretation of the two. . . . *Christ's active and passive obedience should be regarded as complementary parts of an organic whole* [italics mine]."[35]

If the active and passive aspects of Christ's obedience cannot be separated, if they are complementary parts of a whole, and if they are alike vicarious in nature, there seems to be a serious discrepancy and inconsistency with limited atonement. The problem is this, "How is it possible to have a Christ Who lived a substitutionary life, which obviously was not confined or limited to the elect, and at the same time have a Christ whose substitutionary death was only for the elect?" Is it not contradictory to believe in the unlimited vicarious nature of Christ's life and at the same time believe in the limited vicarious nature of His death, since His life and death sufferings "cannot be separated"?

VII. *The Necessity of Faith for Salvation*

This is the most serious problem with the limited view. Even though those who accept the limited view pay lip service to the need for faith, the fact remains that if their view of the design of the atonement is true, faith is meaningless and without purpose. Owen is a good example of one who acknowledges the

---

[35] Berkhof, *op. cit.*, pp. 180, 181.

necessity of faith and yet in the final analysis removes it as a real condition of salvation. "If the fruits of the death of Christ be to be communicated unto us upon a condition, and that condition to be among those fruits, and be itself to be absolutely communicated upon no condition, then all the fruits of the death of Christ are as absolutely procured for them for whom he died as if no condition had been prescribed; for these things come all to one. . . . Faith, which is this condition, is itself procured by the death of Christ for them for whom he died, to be freely bestowed on them, without the prescription of any such condition as on whose fulfilling the collation of it should depend."[36] This is a rather involved statement which in essence declares that Christ procured the condition of faith for the elect, thus removing every condition for salvation from them. One would wish for scriptural support for such an observation. The truth of the matter is there simply is no scriptural support for the idea that Christ purchased faith for the elect, thus removing the condition of salvation for them. The Bible insists everywhere that before ever man's sin is put away he must believe on the name of the only begotten Son of God: ". . . And that believing ye might have life through his name" (John 20:31). If faith does not remain as a condition of salvation for men, then words have lost all their meaning.

Questions regarding the limited view may be stated in various ways. If the cross applies its own benefits and is God's only saving instrumentality, what place does faith have? When are man's sins forgiven—at the cross, thus before multitudes of men are ever born, or when man believes and thus appropriates what Christ has done? Paul said forgiveness comes to the individual when he believes: "Be it known unto you therefore, men and brethren, that through this man is preached unto you the forgiveness of sins: And by him all *that believe are justified from all things,* from which ye could not be justified by the law of Moses" (Acts 13:38, 39). This is the universal testimony of Scripture. There is no exception; the cross is never said to apply its own benefits.

---

[36] Owen, *op. cit.*, X, p. 450.

Does not the strict limited view of the atonement also weaken the doctrine of total depravity? If Christ's death secured the salvation of the elect and if it saves and applies its own benefits, how can the elect be said to be born totally depraved or without any merit before God? In the limited view all the elect have all the merit of the Savior by virtue of His death alone. "It is a plenteous redemption, full and complete. Men are not merely brought into a state where they can be saved, but they are actually saved by it. Through it, God is not merely made reconcilable to them, but the redeemed are actually reconciled to God. Salvation is not conditionally obtained for them, but absolutely."[37] There seems to be a contradiction among these claims as to what saves and when that salvation is a reality and the Apostle Peter's testimony: "To him give all the prophets witness, that through his name whosoever believeth in him shall receive remission of sins" (Acts 10:43).

Nothing is clearer in Scripture than that until men believe they are lost in the broadest sense of that term. The elect are just as lost as the nonelect, until they believe. In Ephesians 2:3, they are said to be ". . . by nature the children of wrath, even as others." Thus, the work of Christ even for the elect is provisional and dependent upon their acceptance of it by faith. Granted, this faith which the elect must exercise is not a work, or something which improves the work of Christ; yet they must do the believing, and until they do, and unless they do, they are lost.

Men in their unregenerate state are not distinguished in the Bible. The elect and the nonelect are both viewed as lost and in need of Christ. But those who restrict the death of Christ to the elect are forced to make just such a distinction between lost sinners who are elect and lost sinners who are not elect.

The basis for the limited view that Christ's death saves is found in those passages which speak of His work as complete. The unlimited redemptionists in no way deny these. We cannot emphasize too strongly the fact of Scripture that Christ's death completely satisfied the righteous demands of God and was a

---

[37] Gill, *op. cit.*, p. 30.

complete substitution. What the limited redemptionist fails to do is take into consideration that whole host of other passages which show the necessity of individual appropriation of that finished work by faith.

Crawford's statements in this connection will put the limited view clearly before us. Speaking of the death of Christ he said: "For while it provides a suitable and sufficient remedy for all the evils and miseries of our sinful state, it also obtains that grace of the Holy Spirit by which this remedy is effectually applied to those who are made partakers of its benefits. Thus, does it not only *put them in a saveable position* or place salvation, as it were, within their reach but it secures salvation for them, and *actually 'saves them to the uttermost.'* "[38]

The point of conflict in the limited view becomes apparent when one observes what this same writer in the same work has to say about the relation of faith to salvation. After quoting many of the choice passages which show the absolute necessity of faith for the appropriation of Calvary's accomplishments, he says: ". . . Invitations must be complied with, promises must be relied on, and proffered blessings must be received by us, in order that we may be personally benefited by them. . . . Food will not nourish us unless we partake of it; a remedy will not cure us unless we consent to have it applied; and no more will Christ, with all His fulness of spiritual blessings, be to us personally of any real advantage, unless we receive and rest upon Him for salvation."[39] With equal force the same writer again declares: "Faith in Christ is expressly declared in Scripture to be the means by which we become partakers of His purchased blessings."[40]

This insistence upon the fact that the cross saves and at the same time upon the necessity of faith by limited redemptionists is not some isolated view; it is shared by many.

Smeaton said of the nature of the atonement: ". . . The atonement, as a fact in history, is as replete with saving results

[38] Crawford, *op. cit.,* pp. 121, 122.
[39] *Ibid.,* p. 145.
[40] *Ibid.,* p. 509.

and consequences, as the fall of man. . . ."[41] Concerning the relation of faith to this he said, ". . . It is the means by which redemption is appropriated. . . . Without it there is no relation to Jesus, and the atonement would be offered in vain."[42]

Accepting these two facts—the cross saves and the necessity of faith—changes the design of the atonement from an actual one which applies its own benefits to a provisional one requiring faith for the appropriation of its results. There seems to be a glaring conflict in saying on the one hand that the death of Christ "secures" and "guarantees" the salvation of the elect and that it saves them and, on the other hand, that faith is necessary to apply the benefits. The question is, "Was the redemptive work of Christ actual apart from other considerations or was it potential, requiring faith to apply its benefits?" This question concerns the divine design of the atonement which we discussed earlier. It does not seem that limited redemptionists can have it both ways. Either the atonement was provisional or it was not.

We have been arguing for the provisional nature of the atonement and thus against the idea that the cross applies its own benefits and that it in itself "saves unto the uttermost." The point of conflict boils down to this: If the divine design of the atonement is what limited redemptionists say it is, then how can it be at the same time provisional and "offered in vain" if men do not believe it? For the limited redemptionists to say it is provisional militates against their dogmatic assertions regarding its design or nature and places them in the position of the modified Calvinists or unlimited redemptionists who have always argued for its provisional nature and potential power toward the sinner.

The difficulty is not lessened, as the limited redemptionist supposes, by saying that faith and the work of the Holy Spirit were included in the accomplishments of the cross. The modified Calvinist also rejects the idea that faith comes apart from the Spirit's work or that it adds one iota to the completed and vicar-

[41] George Smeaton, *The Doctrine of the Atonement as Taught by Christ Himself* (Grand Rapids: Zondervan Publishing House, 1953), p. 366.
[42] *Ibid.*, pp. 396, 398.

ious sacrifice of Christ. He does stand on Biblical ground, however, when he insists on the necessity of the exercise of that faith in order to appropriate the provisional work of Calvary. The point at issue is not related to the absolute finality of the sacrifice of Christ nor to the totality of its scope. The crux of the matter concerns the problem of whether or not the sacrifice was provisional in nature. The simple fact of the admission of the necessity of faith—regardless of the source of that faith—makes the atonement provisional and potential and not immediate and actual in the application of its benefits. The subject of the source and nature of the faith which man places in Christ is a matter not directly related to the discussion at hand.

This whole problem is complicated even more for the limited redemptionist when he insists, as Owen does, that the sin of unbelief has no particular significance. In a quotation which we used earlier[43] Owen said regarding unbelief: ". . . Is it a sin or not? If not, why should they be punished for it? If it be, then Christ underwent the punishment due to it, or not. If so, then why must that hinder more than their other sins for which he died, from partaking of the fruit of his death?"[44]

This logic militates against two of the most basic scriptural principles. First, it removes the necessity for belief and all the importance from belief. Second, it postulates the absurd idea that unbelief on the part of the unsaved is not a sin for which he should be punished since Christ died for it.

If the sin of unbelief is to be viewed as all other sins and is to be included as one for which Christ removed all penalty, there does not seem to be any reason for faith. Believing that Christ's death paid for the sin of the rejection of His person and work means that for whomever He died there is salvation whether they believe or not. Since in the strict Calvinistic scheme of things it is not a sin to disbelieve, it is legitimate to ask why God demands faith and repentance of all men (Acts 17:30). Following this line of reasoning, faith is altogether unnecessary, totally irrelevant and without any real purpose; even if the elect do not believe, they will still be saved since Christ died for

---

[43] See chapter four.
[44] Owen, *op. cit.*, X, p. 174.

their unbelief. Nothing could be more contrary to the Scriptures than that.

To sum up the limited view regarding the relation of faith to salvation, it may be said that it holds men are lost and destined to spend eternity apart from God because they were born in sin, were not elect, hence not included in Christ's death. The Bible, on the other hand, declares that men are lost because of their refusal to receive God's provision for their sin. The issue is no longer a question of sin alone but the question of man's relationship to the Son of God. In the limited view, the sin of unbelief cannot be charged to the nonelect, for no salvation and no Savior have been provided for them. Thus, in the limited view, the nonelect are not guilty of their rejection of Christ, for they have no Christ to reject; whereas in the unlimited and, we believe, Biblical view men are guilty before God and will be condemned on the basis of their rejection of Christ.

VIII. *The Convicting Work of the Holy Spirit*

Believing in limited redemption seems not only to remove the importance, if not the necessity, of faith but also to raise a question as to the necessity and possibility of any work of the Holy Spirit for the nonelect.

By necessity, if Christ died only for the elect, then the work of the Holy Spirit which must find its origin and basis in that death must also be confined to the elect. This means that the Holy Spirit has never had a ministry to the nonelect in the world either before or since Christ's death. The Holy Spirit's work could not reach out beyond the elect if the death of Christ did not have this universal scope since the Spirit's ministry was procured in and through the cross. In other words, how could a part of the work of Christ on the cross be universal if the whole of it was not? The difficulty in this connection with the limited view is much the same as was discovered in the attempt to apply "natural" benefits from the cross to the nonelect while restricting the "spiritual" benefits to the elect.

The problem really centers in the convicting work of the Holy Spirit since this is His principal ministry toward the unsaved. How can the Spirit be said to have a ministry toward the entire world in showing all men their need of Christ if the death of Christ did not reach to the entire world? Furthermore, what need is there for the convicting work of the Spirit toward the elect if the cross applies its own benefits? It even seems unnecessary for the Spirit to regenerate the elect at a point in time if the death of Christ has already done it. On the one hand, why would the Spirit convict the elect of the sin of rejecting Christ if Christ's death paid for their sin of unbelief? On the other hand, how could the Spirit convict the nonelect if they have no relationship and therefore no responsibility to Christ's death?

The interpretation which limited redemptionists place upon John 16:8-11 is very revealing of the dilemma they face in this regard. The passage delineates the threefold work of the Holy Spirit in the world and reads as follows: "And when he is come, he will reprove the world of sin, and of righteousness, and of judgment: Of sin, because they believe not on me; Of righteousness, because I go to my Father, and ye see me no more; Of judgment, because the prince of this world is judged."

A normal reading of this passage leads one to understand that Christ was here informing the disciples of a threefold ministry of the Holy Spirit to the entire world. This is precisely how John Calvin understood the passage. "Under the term *world* are, I think, included not only those who would be truly converted to Christ, but hypocrites and reprobates."[45]

Not all of Calvin's espoused followers share his view of this passage, though. For example, Pink says: "But, it may be said, is not the present mission of the Holy Spirit to 'convict *the world* of sin'? And we answer, It is not. The *mission* of the Spirit is threefold; to glorify Christ, to vivify the elect, to edify the saints. John 16:8-11 does not describe the 'mission' of the Spirit, but sets forth the *significance* of His *presence* here in the world. It treats not of His subjective work in sinners, showing them their need of Christ, by searching their consciences and

---

[45] John Calvin, *Commentary on the Gospel According to John* (Grand Rapids: Wm. B. Eerdmans Publishing Co., 1949), p. 138.

striking terror to their hearts; what we have there is entirely objective."[46]

Again, the same writer emphasizes his point: "We repeat, John 16:8-11 makes no reference to the *mission* of the Spirit of God in the world, for during this dispensation, the Spirit has no mission and ministry worldward. . . ."[47]

Another explains the word *world* used here as referring to the Jews of that day who rejected Christ. "The *world* here spoken of as thus convinced, reproved, and condemned of the Spirit primarily refers to the Jews, who in the times of this outpouring of the Spirit would be convinced of their deep and aggravated sin in rejecting Jesus Christ."[48] Having thus limited the ministry of the Spirit to the world of the Jews, Owen has second thoughts and admits, "But while this is primarily spoken of the Jews, it is in the highest degree true of all who have heard the name of Christ. The office of the Spirit is to convince them of sin in refusing to believe in an offered Redeemer, and to reprove and condemn them for this state of apathy and unbelief."[49]

Serious questions are raised when a limited redemptionist concedes that the Spirit's convicting ministry is upon all who have heard the name of Christ. This of course does not make the ministry completely worldwide but at least it is sure to include at least some for whom Christ did not die. How is this possible when the Spirit's work spoken of in this context by our Lord was based squarely upon His death? This is true not only in the general context of the Upper Room Discourse but it is also true in the immediate context as well. The three indictments which the Spirit is said to level against the world are all based for their very validity upon the finished work of Christ on the cross.

Buswell, who believes in limited atonement, acknowledges that it is the death of Christ which ". . . furnishes the ethical

---

[46] Pink, *op. cit.*, p. 92.

[47] *Ibid.*, p. 94.

[48] John J. Owen, *A Commentary on the Gospel of John* (New York: Charles Scribner & Co., 1886), p. 385.

[49] *Ibid.*

and logical ground for common grace. . . .[50] He then goes on to say, "In my opinion the convicting work of the Holy Spirit in the world in general is a work upon the hearts of all men prior to either faith or regeneration, a work wherein not only is the Gospel freely offered to all, but all are brought to a point of enablement to such a degree that, if having been convicted, they reject the grace of God thus offered to them, they are subject to the eternal wrath and curse of God. . . ."[51]

It is difficult to conceive of a God Who would through the death of His Son not only make a universal offer of salvation to all men but who would also through the Holy Spirit bring all men to see their need of Christ if His Son did not in the first place provide a redemption for all.

The question therefore is, "Since the Spirit's work was based on Christ's work, on what basis could the Holy Spirit bring conviction to men who were beyond the scope of Christ's death?" Another troublesome question is presented in this regard. Owen and other limited redemptionists admit that the sin of which the Holy Spirit is here said to convince or give demonstrable proof of is the sin of unbelief in Christ.[52] Does it not appear strange that the Holy Spirit would bring such conviction to those who could not reject Christ since, if the limited point of view be allowed, He did not do anything for them which they could reject. No one can reject something which was never even intended for him nor extended to him in the first place.

Now concerning the extent of this promised convicting ministry of the Spirit, there can be no doubt but that it is worldwide. This is true for a number of reasons beyond the fact that the word *cosmos,* "world," is used by the Lord.

Christ was dealing with discouraged and defeated disciples because of the prospect of His imminent death. He had just commissioned them to be witnesses after His departure, in a world that would be hostile and antagonistic to them and the One they were to preach (John 15:18-25). It was because of their own

---

[50] James Oliver Buswell, *A Systematic Theology of the Christian Religion* (Grand Rapids: Zondervan Publishing House, 1963), II, pp. 142, 143.
[51] *Ibid.,* p. 157.
[52] *Ibid.,* p. 386.

inadequacies and the world's antagonism that the Savior promised them the Spirit's aid. They were not going to be left alone as orphans; the Holy Spirit would be their Comforter (John 15:26—16:6). Since they were to bear testimony to all men and not just the elect, and since they would be enabled to do this by the Holy Spirit, His ministry would then also be to all men.

The threefold indictment of the Spirit upon the world does not mean the world would thus receive the Christ of whom the Spirit was bearing testimony. That is not implied in the word "convince." What is involved, though, is rebuke which brings conviction or acknowledgment of what has been done. The Spirit of God had done this work before (Gen. 6:3), but now after the Son's departure He was to perform a more intensive work because of the Savior's absence. He was to give demonstrable proof to all men of the facts about sin because they do not believe, about righteousness because the only righteous One has been crucified and raised from the dead, and about judgment because the prince of the world was judged, thus assuring the future judgment of all his followers.

The present ministry of the Spirit in the world is the answer of the Lord's petition to the Father: "Neither pray I for these alone, but for them also which shall believe on me through their word; That they all may be one; as thou, Father, art in me, and I in thee, that they also may be one in us: *that the world may believe that thou hast sent me . . . . that the world may know that thou has sent me, and hast loved them, as thou hast loved me* [italics mine]" (John 17:20-23). In accordance with the Savior's request, it is the third person of the Godhead who uses the believer's dedicated life and the Word of God to bring the world to an acknowledgment that the Son was sent by the Father Who loved them. Of course, they do not all believe, but they are all without excuse.

Another difficulty in the limited redemption concept becomes apparent in this connection. The necessity for this universal convicting ministry of the Spirit in common grace lies in the spiritual blindness which Satan brings upon men. That blindness which is part of man's total inability is not true only of the elect. It is true of all men, and therefore the Spirit's ministry must be coextensive with Satan's imposed blindness. Then, too, one wonders about the nature of this spiritual blindness. Paul declared, ". . . The god of this world hath blinded the minds of them which believe not, lest the light of the glorious gospel of Christ, who is the image of God, should shine unto them" (2 Cor. 4:4). If Christ did not die for the nonelect, of what are they blinded? It cannot be that they are blinded of Christ's death for them and their need for faith if Christ never died for them. They cannot be blinded in their unbelief because they have nothing to believe or to disbelieve since they have no relationship to Christ's death!

The difficulty of explaining such a passage is removed when it is acknowledged that spiritual darkness has come upon all men, making it impossible for them to understand or believe that Christ died for them. The Holy Spirit works through various means to bring blinded sinners to the realization of their need and Christ's provision. This He does for all men even though many resist and refuse His work (Gen. 6:3; Prov. 1:24-26; Isa. 63:10; Acts 7:51).

IX. *Adam and Christ*

According to Romans 5:12, it was by one man, and all men in him, that sin and death entered the world: "Wherefore, as by one man sin entered into the world, and death by sin; and so death passed upon all men, for that all have sinned." It seems clear from this text that Adam was not only the federal head of the entire human race but that he was also the natural head; and thus when he committed the sin, the whole race being represented by him and being seminally in him, committed the sin also. Therefore Paul could say, "for that all have sinned," meaning by it that all sinned at a point in time in the past, namely, when Adam sinned.

Further evidence for the actual participation of all mankind in the sin, and therefore the universal diffusion of the result of that sin, follows in Romans 5:13, 14: "(For until the law sin was in the world: but sin is not imputed when there is no law. Nevertheless death reigned from Adam to Moses, even over

them that had not sinned after the similitude of Adam's transgression, who is the figure of him that was to come." Physical
death reigned as a tyrant over men from Adam to Moses even
though law had not yet been codified in that period and even
though men did not reenact the same sin that Adam had committed. Since death did not exist before Adam's transgression
but was a result and punishment for his sin, and yet since men
died after Adam who had not sinned in exactly the same way, it
can only follow that those who thus died did so because they
were participants in Adam's sin and therefore recipients of his
subsequent punishment.

There need be no doubt about the fact that Adam was a
type of Christ since he is called "the figure of him that was to
come" (Rom. 5:14). Adam was such a figure or type because, as
he became through his one act of disobedience the cause of death
to his descendants, so Christ became through His one act of
obedience the dispenser of righteousness and the cause of eternal
life to as many as receive Him in faith (Rom. 5:17).

While the apostle's chief concern in Romans 5:12-19 is to
show how a single act of one affects many, he nevertheless reveals a likeness as well as several contrasts between Adam and
Christ. "The likeness consists in this: *one man* is the source
of sin, death, condemnation—*one man* the source of righteousness
and life. Again, *one act* is the evil source—*one act* the good
source."[53]

The first difference between the first and last Adam is to be
found in the phrase, "But not as the offence, so also is the free
gift" (Rom. 5:15). Adam's "offense" brought sin and death to
himself as well as to the entire human race of which he was the
natural and representative head. In direct contrast, Christ's
"free gift," or more literally "gracious gift," was not for Himself
at all but exclusively for others.

There is another difference indicated in the same verse
in the words "much more." The thought is that Christ's one
act is more certain of having its effect upon "the many" than

---

[53] R. C. H. Lenski, *The Interpretation of St. Paul's Epistle to the Romans*
(Columbus: Wartburg Press, 1945), p. 367.

Adam's one act had upon the same group. Surely there is a greater abundance of grace and life in Christ than there was of death in Adam; yet Paul does not seem to be emphasizing either a contrast of *quality* between life and death or a contrast of *quantity*—a greater amount of life than of death. It is rather a higher degree of certainty which the apostle wishes to stress. Hodge has correctly said the words "much more" do ". . . not express a higher degree of efficacy, but of evidence of certainty: 'If one thing has happened, *much more* certainly may the other be relied upon.' "[54] Another Greek exegete adds a fitting word: "The apostle is not at all concerned to demonstrate that there is more grace in Christ than there was death in Adam. What he wishes to prove is that if a slight cause could bring sentence of death on all mankind, this same mankind will experience in its entirety the salutary effect of a much more powerful cause."[55]

The Romans 5 passage relates to the extent of the atonement, especially in verses 15-19. Though the definite article does not appear in the English translation, it is present in the Greek text before the word "many" in both instances in verse 15. Therefore, it should read "the many" thus referring to the same group in the case of Adam and of Christ.

By this phrase, "the many," Paul is speaking of the entire human race just as much as if he had said "all." The definite article which appears before the word "many" proves this. No doubt the reason for his choice of "the many" instead of "all" was to provide a better contrast to the "one" from which the sin went forth and the "one" from which the grace went forth. The term "all" would be more opposed to the word "some" than it would to "one."

Needless to say, this passage creates serious problems for the one believing in limited atonement. Paul's emphasis is clearly that to the totality of the race was grace extended through one man, Jesus Christ. Nothing could be more contradictory to the limited view than that.

---

[54] Charles Hodge, *Commentary on the Epistle to the Romans* (Philadelphia: Alfred Martien, 1873), p. 257.

[55] F. Godet, *Commentary on St. Paul's Epistle to the Romans* (New York: Funk & Wagnalls, 1883), p. 216.

Godet, a Greek exegete and theologian, put it this way: "What the apostle here compares is not as some have thought, the abundance of the effects, but rather the *degree of extension* belonging to the two works; for the emphasis is on the term *the many*, of the two sides of the parallel; and this degree of extension he measures very logically according to the degree of abundance in the factors—a degree indicated on the one side by the subordinate clause of the first proposition; *through the offence of one,* on the other by the subject of the second; *the grace of God, and the gift through this grace of one man.* From the contrast between these factors it is easy to arrive at this conclusion. If from the first factor, so insignificant in a way—the offence of one!—there could go forth an action which spread over the whole multitude of mankind, will not the conclusion hold *a fortiori* that from the two factors acting on the opposite side, so powerful and rich as they are, there must result an action, the *extension* of which shall not be less than that of the first factor, and shall consequently also reach the whole of that multitude."[56]

If "the many" associated with Adam are "the many" unto whom Christ's grace abounded, does this not mean the whole human race will be saved? The answer is an emphatic no! The apostle argues strongly here for the necessity of faith on the part of each of "the many" to whom Christ's grace abounds in order that the grace may be appropriated.

He speaks first of all in verse 15 of the last Adam's work as a grace-gift, which surely implies that it must be received individually. Then, in verse 16 when he says, ". . . The free gift is of many offences unto justification," he does not use the definite article with "many" as he did twice in verse 15.

"The accepters are not the *totality* of men condemned to die; Paul does not even say that they are necessarily numerous. His thought here is arrested by *each* of them, whatever shall be their number."[57] Thus there is on the side of grace a totally different position as compared with those on the side of sin. Those

---

[56] *Ibid.,* p. 214.
[57] *Ibid.,* p. 222.

represented in the sin of Adam and its subsequent judgment did not need to do any more to be condemned. Those who are said to be dead in verse 15 are the same ones under judgment and condemnation in verse 16. But that same group, "the many," must do something about the provision of Christ if they are to be justified. Christ's one act in death made the grace abound to the entire race; it overflowed as the contents of a container filled to overflowing. But it is man's personal reception of that grace poured out at the cross which brings the justification to that part of "the many" which believe.

According to verse 17, it was through Adam's one offence that death reigned but much more those who receive the grace given by the last Adam shall reign in life through Him. The emphasis is upon the necessity of *receiving* the grace. Lenski summarizes this point very well: "The fact that the condemnatory verdict damned all men is beyond question after considering v. 12-15. The fact that the justifying verdict does *not* justify all men ought to be equally beyond question in view of v. 17 and of all that Paul has said regarding justification *by faith alone.*"[58]

The verb in verse 17 translated "receive" signifies literally "the receivers" or "accepters." The word from which this verb comes means "to take," "to lay hold of" or "to receive." Here it obviously refers to an act of faith or acceptance. Godet again comments: "Vv 16 and 17 demonstrate the full reality and quickening efficacy of the *personal application* which every believer makes of the justification obtained by Christ. Affirmed in ver. 16, this individual efficacy is proved in ver. 17. One single agent, serving as the instrument of a very weak cause, could bring about the death of so many individuals who had not *personally* taken part in his act. Consequently, and *much more certainly*, will each of those same individuals, by personally appropriating a force *far superior* in action to the preceding, become thereby a possessor of life."[59]

---
[58] Lenski, *op. cit.*, p. 374.
[59] Godet, *op. cit.*, p. 223.

That all will not receive the extended grace procured for them by Christ seems certain from the fact so clearly stated that they who do shall "reign in life by one, Jesus Christ." Thus, not only does verse 15 support an atonement coextensive with the fall, but verse 17 also implies that some for whom grace abounded will not receive it. Nothing could be more certain from these verses than that all to whom the free gift of righteousness and grace is extended are not receivers.

Other interesting differences of a more technical nature between the judgment and condemnation of Adam's sin and the gracious gift of justification to life issuing from Christ's death are found in verses 18 and 19. These differences or contrasts argue strongly against any worldwide justification in this passage.

Verse 18 is the summation of the teaching in verses 12-17. "Therefore as by the offence of one *judgment came* upon all men to condemnation; even so by the righteousness of one *the free gift came* upon all men unto justification of life" [italics mine]. There are no verbs in the verse in the Greek text; translators and commentators have inserted them. Evidence against any kind of universal justification or even justification apart from faith is found in the word translated "justification" at the close of the verse. In direct contrast to several other words from verse 16 on, which have an ending which emphasizes the end result, this word has an ending which stresses not result at all but action. Perhaps it would be clearer if we took the word translated "judgment" in verse 18 as an example of the contrast. This word with its suffix speaks of a resultant judgment upon all men through Adam that is absolutely final and which will without any further activity on the part of those involved result in condemnation. Yet in the same verse, when Paul speaks of the work of Christ extending the gracious gift of justification unto life to "all men," he uses a suffix or ending on the word justification which does not imply absoluteness in the sense that those thus involved, "all men," are automatically justified. No, his ending has the sense of action but not the result of that action.

Robertson, in his advanced Greek grammar, says: "It is important to seek the meaning not only of the root, but of this formative suffix also when possible." He further states that *ma* denotes result and *sis* means action.[60]

Lenski adds this clarifying statement in his exegesis of the verse: "The difference in the terms is marked: not for all men as for Christ, *dikaioma,* a justifying verdict as the finished and permanent result, but *dikaiosis,* the action of declaring righteous, the action that is repeated in every case in which 'the gift of the righteousness is received' (v. 17) by faith. Adam's fall (result, *paraptoma*) = for all men, *katakrima,* finished condemnation, a result, not merely *katakrisis,* condemning action that occurs in a succession of cases; Christ's *dikaioma,* finished result like Adam's *paraptoma* = for all men, not also *dikaioma,* finished result, but *dikaiosis,* justifying action that occurs in a succession of cases."[61]

Further explanation of the two facts paralleled in verse 18 is given in verse 19. "For as by one man's disobedience many were made sinners, so by the obedience of one shall many be made righteous" (Rom. 5:19). Here again we have the appearance of "the many" which occurred in verse 15 and which was substituted for "all men" in verse 18. The significance of the verse in relation to the extent of the atonement lies in the future "shall many be made righteous" as opposed to the aorist "were made sinners." The aorist tense in Greek stresses point action in the past. It would seem that if two aorists were necessary in verse 18, "judgment *came*" and "the free gift *came,*" two aorists should also appear in verse 19, "many made sinners" and "many made righteous." This, however, is not the case, and because it is not we have a good argument against worldwide justification to parallel worldwide condemnation. Instead of two aorist tenses there is one aorist signifying the finality of the past act of Adam whereby "the many" were constituted sinners. In the case of Christ's act of obedience and its relation to "the many," a future tense appears. The total number involved in Adam's disobedience is not the same as those who shall be constituted righteous. As this entire context and rest of Scripture shows,

[60] A. T. Robertson, *A Grammar of the Greek New Testament in the Light of Historical Research* (Nashville: Broadman Press, 1934), p. 151.

[61] Lenski, *op. cit.,* p. 379.

faith is necessary for the individual application of that procured righteousness. "This passage refers, as is proved by the future *will be made righteous,* to the effectual *application.*"[62]

The idea expressed here is that all along as men receive the abundance of grace and the gift of righteousness, they shall be constituted righteous. " 'The many' with reference to whom the aorist is used are determined by that aorist, 'the many' with reference to whom the future tense is used are limited by that tense. These tenses decide the issue. Christ's obedience will never constitute an unbeliever who spurns this vicarious obedience *dikaios* 'righteous,' declared so by the eternal Judge."[63]

It should be evident from this survey of Romans 5:12-19 that the contrast and comparison of Adam and Christ in this passage lends no support to limited atonement. Through Adam's one act of disobedience the entire human race became the recipients of sin, and through one act of obedience the last Adam brought the gracious gift of righteousness to the entire human race. The disobedience of the one was coextensive with the obedience of the other. "The many" unto whom death came are "the many" unto whom the gracious gift abounded through Christ. There is no clearer passage than this to teach the imputation (putting over to one's account) of Adam's sin to the race and the sin of the race to Christ.

Understandably, those who believe in limited atonement find it necessary to confine "the many" unto whom grace abounded (v. 15) and the "all men" unto whom justification of life came (v. 18) to the elect. The limitation is placed only upon those associated with Christ's work and not upon those associated with Adam's sin, even though the two are parallel in the text.

Hodge, in defense of the strict Calvinistic and limited view, cites the timeworn arguments concerning the frequent limitations upon the words "all," etc., in Scripture. He concludes from this and from the fact that even in the case of Adam's transgression Christ was excepted, and therefore absolutely all did not die in

---

[62] Godet. *op. cit.,* p. 226.
[63] Lenski, *op. cit.,* p. 383.

him, that the work of Christ was not coextensive with the sin of Adam.[64]

Murray brings the same one-sided limitations to the text seemingly to avoid universalism or worldwide justification.[65] It is certainly true that the Bible does not teach that all men will eventually be saved either here or elsewhere. Within this very text itself, as we have demonstrated in the previous pages, the necessity of faith is clearly taught. There is no necessity to place limitations upon one side of the obvious parallel in order to avoid universalism. That false doctrine is repudiated by the apostle both here and elsewhere. He made it as clear as words could make it that, even though the work of the last Adam reached to the same group as that reached by the sin of the first Adam, there is a difference in how the effects of each reach men. Christ's work was a gracious gift implying the need of reception; Adam's sin was not. Christ's gift of righteousness must be received before it is applied to the individual; Adam's sin must not. Christ's obedience shall constitute many righteous, as they believe; Adam's disobedience constituted all men as sinners immediately at the time Adam sinned.

No greater confidence is needed for the proclaimer of the gospel to lost men than that Christ, the last Adam (1 Cor. 15:22, 45), finished a work through which salvation was provided for every single member of the first Adam's condemned race.

X. *The Resurrection of the Wicked Dead*

Another evidence that all men were involved in Christ's work on the cross relates to the resurrection power which His death procured for the entire race. His victory over death provides a basis for the future resurrection not only of the saved but also of the unsaved.

Before Adam sinned, there was no death. As a punishment for sin, death entered the universe in three forms. Man died spiritually; that is, his fellowship with God was immediately

---

[64] Hodge, *op. cit.,* pp. 268, 269.
[65] John Murray, *The Epistle to the Romans* (Grand Rapids: Wm. B. Eerdmans Publishing Co., 1959), I, pp. 191-206.

broken. Man also began to die physically in fulfillment of God's threat: ". . . In the day that thou eatest thereof thou shalt surely die" (Gen. 2:17). One needs only to read God's obituary column in chapter 5 where the phrase "and he died" occurs eight times for proof of physical death resulting from sin. Likewise, man became the subject of spiritual death—eternal separation from God—unless the divine provision of substitution for sin be accepted.

As the last Adam (1 Cor. 15:45), Christ defeated the power of death incurred by the first Adam; and since the penalty of death extended to all men, Christ's victory over death, proved by His own resurrection, must also be the basis for the future resurrection of all men. That all men will be raised was clearly taught by Christ Himself. "Marvel not at this: for the hour is coming, in the which all that are in the graves shall hear his voice, And shall come forth; they that have done good, unto the resurrection of life; and they that have done evil, unto the resurrection of damnation" (John 5:28, 29). It is clear from the immediate context of these verses that the source of resurrection power as well as the authority to execute judgment resides in the Son of Man as a gift from the Father (John 5:19-27).

"The abrogating of death is no less than a repeal of the sentence that was given in Eden, except for the abiding spiritual aspects of death; and is brought about not only by a divine decree which determines its end, but by a universal resurrection or renewal of all that physical death hath wrought. This reference to the cessation of the reign of death, as presented in 1 Corinthians 15:26, is in connection with the *end* or final resurrection-event which closes the whole program of resurrection which began with Christ's resurrection and includes the resurrection of those that are Christ's at His coming and includes, also, this, the end resurrection when the remaining dead will 'stand' before the great white throne (Rev. 20:12)."[66]

Whatever view of last things one accepts, premillennial, postmillennial or amillennial, the fact remains that all men will be raised. Neither is it of any consequence to the present discus-

---

[66] Chafer, *op. cit.*, II, p. 154.

sion whether the church and Israel are raised at the same time or at different times or whether there is a single general resurrection or a resurrection in stages. All evangelicals must agree that all men will be raised from the dead in the future.

The wicked dead are just as much a part of the resurrection program as are the righteous dead. And both will be raised by the power of Christ's resurrection. This being true, it must be admitted that even the nonelect were included in the Savior's death since it is on the basis of His death that they shall one day be resurrected to live a conscious existence forever.

But in the limited atonement concept, the nonelect are not included in Christ's death. If they are not, then how is it that the source of power for their future resurrection is to be found in Christ's defeat of death by His own death and resurrection? There is no other alternative; the basis of the future resurrection and judgment of all unsaved men finds its source squarely in the death and resurrection of Christ.

CONCLUSION

It is difficult to be objective when dealing with a subject about which one has firm convictions and over which evangelical scholarship is divided. However, every effort has been made to be fair in our consideration of the Bible's testimony of the extent of the atonement.

Our study of the Biblical evidence has brought us to solid evidence for the substitutionary nature of Christ's death. His vicarious death on the cross was the complete and final satisfaction of all the demands of the offended righteousness of the Father. The sufficiency of that work of the Son remains whether it be accepted by the sinner or not. Man's reception of the purchased redemption does not add one iota to it, but merely appropriates its great accomplishments, thus bringing the results of it to the receiver. The Father is perfectly satisfied with the Son's work on the cross, and He proved it when He raised Him from the dead.

Taking all the Scripture bearing upon the subject into consideration, it must be said that the divine purpose in the atonement was to *provide* redemption, reconciliation and propitiation for all men. The cross is not the only saving instrument in the Father's plan of redemption, for apart from faith it saves no one. Salvation is impossible without the cross, and so is it impossible without faith.

Believing that Christ died for all men produces no difficulty with Scripture which specifies His death for the elect. The Biblical extent of the atonement is settled by answering the question of the Father's purpose in the death of His Son. If His purpose was to justify all those for whom Christ died apart from any other consideration, then of course He died only for some because all will not be saved. However, if the Father's purpose was to *provide* a redemption for all which was dependent upon faith for its personal application, then His death must be extended to all. The Bible surely speaks of a completed work, an absolute salvation secured by Christ; but it speaks with equal emphasis of the absolute necessity of faith before any of the benefits of Calvary are personalized.

We have tried to face squarely the problems on both sides of the question. The solutions presented may not satisfy everyone; but if what has been said will stimulate more Bible study on the subject, it will have been well worth the effort. The author finds deep and perplexing difficulties with the limited view. He must grant that limited atonement is quite consistent with the other points of Calvinism, but he is more convinced than ever that it is irreconcilable with the whole of Scripture.

What confidence for the soul winner to know that the Savior has not only commissioned His servants to take the gospel to all men but has also taught that His purpose in coming into the world was to call "sinners to repentance" (Luke 5:32) and to "seek and to save that which was lost" (Luke 19:10). Unless only the elect are "sinners," and unless they are the only ones who constitute the "lost," it must be admitted that according to Christ's own testimony His death reached out beyond the elect. Likewise, it is indeed comforting to know that Paul, the greatest missionary who ever lived, apart from Christ, and who gave us more information on the sovereignty of God and election than any other New Testament writer, also extended the benefits of Calvary beyond the elect to include the whole world (2 Cor. 5:17-19).

The death Christ died was a death in the place of all men—a death which accomplished a work that completely satisfied God the Father. It was a death which provided life for every mem-

ber of Adam's lost race who has ever lived or ever shall live—
a death that made it possible for the Father to be just and at the
same time the Justifier of any sinner who does nothing more
than receive Christ as personal Savior.

When I survey the wondrous cross,
On which the Prince of Glory died,
My richest gain I count but loss,
And pour contempt on all my pride.

Forbid it, Lord, that I should boast,
Save in the death of Christ, my God;
All the vain things that' charm me most,
I sacrifice them to His blood.

See, from His head, His hands, His feet,
Sorrow and love flow mingled down;
Did e'er such love and sorrow meet,
Or thorns compose so rich a crown?

Were the whole realm of nature mine,
That were a present far too small;
Love so amazing, so divine,
Demands my soul, my life, my all.

—Isaac Watts

Appendix A

LIMITED ATONEMENT AND SHARING THE GOSPEL

The question of how the gospel can be personalized by those who believe Christ did not die for all was introduced on pages 114–18. There, while exploring the problem of the universal offer of the gospel in limited atonement, it was stated that according to limited redemptionists, "the gospel is not to be personalized but presented in more general terms."[1]

The impossibility of being able to personalize the good news of God's saving grace to sinners raises an enormous theological issue for limited atonement. I want to explore that here.

What Must the Sinner Believe to Be Saved?

The message of personal salvation must include, first, the fact that all stand guilty and condemned before God. Second, it must set forth the Lord Jesus Christ as the only Substitute for sin and sinners. Third, the need for personal faith or trust in Christ alone as the individual's sinbearer is essential. Salvation is all of God from start to finish. Salvation is a gift from God. Salvation is by grace alone through faith alone in Christ alone.

This means there are three absolute essentials in the message of salvation. It must include (1) something about personal sin; (2) the

---

1. Page 117.

substitutionary death of Christ for the sinner; and (3) faith or trust in Christ's finished work. No one can become a child of God unless he acknowledges his lost and condemned position before God. No one can become a child of God unless he believes what the Bible says about the substitutionary death of Christ. And by the same token, no one can become a child of God unless and until he accepts the work of Christ on the cross as a payment for his sin.

Should the Gospel Be Personalized?

Indeed, the good news of God's saving grace must be personalized. No one, for example, can enter the family of God because he acknowledges that his friend is a sinner and guilty. God will not save anyone who refuses to acknowledge his own lost condition before Him. Christ must be received as the Substitute for the individual's sin. The lost person must understand that Christ died for him. No one can possibly become a child of God because he accepted Christ's payment for somebody else's sin. Likewise, it is just as true that the one desiring to become a Christian must exercise faith himself. No one can believe for somebody else.

How Does Limited Atonement Affect Sharing the Gospel?

It is my contention that the person who believes Christ died only for the elect—those who do respond in faith—cannot honestly personalize one of the essentials of the gospel message discussed above. Let me explain this.

First, all those who believe in limited atonement believe each and every person in the world stands condemned outside of Christ. Therefore, they can and do stress emphatically to the person that all, universally, have sinned and fall short of the glory of God and that includes "you." *All*, without exception, not just *all*, without distinction, stand condemned before a holy God. There is none who is righteous, not even one, even among those who believe in limited atonement. This essential of the saving message is most certainly personalized—as it should be, since it is done so in Scripture.

Second, when sharing God's good news to the lost, those who believe Christ died only for the elect should not, if they are consistent and honest, tell the sinner, "Christ died for you." They do not know who the elect are; nobody does except God. Since this is true, the sinner cannot be told Christ died for him and paid his debt of sin.

The usual way of witnessing for Christ from the limited perspective is to follow a pattern something like this: the unsaved person is reminded from Scripture that he is guilty before God, verses of Scripture like Romans 3:9 and 23 are reviewed with the person, and it is stressed that this truth applies to him.

Then the potential convert is told that Christ died for sinners and verses are used to demonstrate this. But the sinner cannot be told, "Christ died for *you.* He paid *your* debt on Calvary." It is essential that generalization comes in. The sinner, of course, has been shown how he is in need of salvation and therefore he assumes when told Christ died for "sinners" and the "lost" that he is included. The one believing in limited atonement allows the sinner to think that, while all along he does not intend that meaning because he does not know whether the person is elect or not.

Third, the limited view is not a hindrance to personalizing the fact that God's gift of salvation must be received by faith by the individual sinner. Limited redemptionists and unlimited redemptionists alike can and do call for the unregenerate to personally place their faith in Christ alone for salvation.

Is It Necessary to Personalize All the Essentials of the Message of Salvation?

As I stressed earlier, I do believe it is essential that *all* three aspects of the gospel should be personalized. I will go one step further and say that unless all three essentials are made personal, salvation does not result.

Everyone on both sides of the extent of the atonement would agree that the person who wants to be sure of heaven must first acknowledge how God views him. Each one must believe he is a helpless, hopeless, condemned sinner in the eyes of God. It will not do to affirm that humankind in general is sinful or even that his worst enemy is sinful. The one seeking salvation stands guilty before God and he must acknowledge it.

It is equally true that all on both sides of the debate agree that the sinner must exercise personal faith or trust in Christ to be saved. No one can believe for someone else. Each one must exercise personal trust in Christ alone as Substitute.

The agreement between the two sides of the atonement's extent stops with these two essentials. On the second essential—the substitutionary death of Christ—the two views are worlds apart. The limited view says

Christ died only for the elect while the unlimited view says He died for all without exception.

What, precisely, is it that brings salvation to the individual person? Is it believing he is a sinner? No. Is it believing Christ died for some sinners with the hope that "some" includes the one believing? No.

What brings a condemned, hopeless, helpless sinner into the family of God is trust and acceptance of Christ's finished work on the cross as payment *for his sin*, the one believing. Since this is true, the sinner needs to be told, "Christ died for you. He paid your dept. Will you accept *His* payment for *your* sins?" The one believing in limited atonement cannot honestly say this since he does not believe Christ died for all. Thus the most essential element of the gospel message must be given with tongue in cheek from the limited perspective.

A Response from a Limited Redemptionist

J. I. Packer is one who believes Christ died only for the elect and has also honestly faced the issue under discussion here. In a section titled "What Is the Evangelistic Message?" he says it is a message about God, about sin, about Christ, and a summons to faith *and* repentance.[2]

Packer's discussion about the sinner's sin is very personalized.

> The gospel is a message about *sin*. It tells *us* how *we* have fallen short of God's standard; how *we* have become guilty, filthy, and helpless in sin, and now stand under the wrath of God. It tells *us* that the reason why *we* sin continually is that *we* are sinners by nature, and that nothing *we* do, or try to do, for ourselves can put us right, or bring us back into God's favour. It shows *us* ourselves as God sees us, and teaches us to think of ourselves as God thinks of us. Thus it leads us to self-despair. And this also is a necessary step. Not till *we* have learned our need to get right with God, and *our* inability to do so by any effort of our own, can *we* come to know the Christ who saves from sin [italics mine except the first one].[3]

Packer makes a deliberate switch from the need to personalize the reality of sin to a generalizing of Christ's death in the place of sinners.

2. J. I. Packer, *Evangelism and the Sovereignty of God* (Chicago: InterVarsity Press, 1961), 58–73.
3. Ibid., 59.

The fact is, the New Testament never calls on any man to repent on the ground that Christ died specifically and particularly for him. The basis on which the New Testament invites sinners to put faith in Christ is simply that they need Him, and that He offers Himself to them, and that those who receive Him are promised all the benefits that His death secured for His people.[4]

I must ask in response to Packer's views, "Why and on what ground do you insist the unregenerate must acknowledge his own sin and guilt before God before he can be made right with God and then in the next breath depersonalize the death of Christ and say the seeker does not need to believe Christ died specifically for him to be saved?"

The biblical and theological bases for Packer's distinction are unpersuasive. The bases must be found; without it the distinction would be out of harmony with and inconsistent with the view that Christ died only for the elect.

The Bible does not tell us to insist that the sinner must believe he is lost and guilty before he can get saved. It simply and repeatedly tells us he is a sinner. That is simply the conclusion Scripture brings us to by its repeated emphasis upon man's sinful condition and his only hope of salvation. For the same reason, it follows that since Christ died to pay for mankind's sin, meaning He took the sinner's place, all who would become children of God must accept God's payment for their sin—the death of Christ for them.

What this all means is that limited atonement runs aground when it comes to sharing the gospel of God's saving grace.

---

4. Ibid., 68.

Appendix B

ROMANS 9:13, 9:22; 1 PETER 2:7-8

When the extent of the atonement is discussed, the subject of predestination, especially what has come to be known as double predestination, often comes up. The three passages usually appealed to in support of double predestination are Romans 9:13 and 9:22 and 1 Peter 2:8.

As the reader of this book has already seen, the book's subject matter is concerned with the extent of the atonement and not the doctrines of election and predestination. These two doctrines are related to the subject of the book but are not to be equated with it. Throughout the book we have sought to answer the question, "For whom did Christ die?" That has been our focus.

The three passages are not directly related to the question this book raises and seeks to answer, but they do have some bearing on the subject.

The issue of predestination often does come up in conjunction with the question of the extent of the atonement. I would therefore like to illustrate that while these three passages are indeed difficult ones, they do not support double predestination, and they certainly do not lend any support to the doctrine of limited atonement.

There are what we might call difficult passages associated with many, if not all, of the major doctrines of Scripture. In dealing with these passages, there are important steps to follow. First, it must be admitted when a text of Scripture seems to teach the opposite of what many clear passages teach. This is what we mean by a problem passage. Second, the interpreter of Scripture must not ignore such a problem passage or attempt to explain it away. Rather, it is incumbent upon the interpreter to determine whether there is a way to harmonize the difficult text with the clear ones. Sometimes, for example, there is more than one legitimate way to understand the grammar and syntax. When that is the case, the way that does not contradict the clear passages is to be adopted.

Third, it is important to always remember the basic rule of hermeneutics or biblical interpretation: A doctrine must not be built on a problem passage. Rather, doctrine is built on the clear passages, and the difficult ones must be understood in light of the clear ones, not the other way around. There may be times when men cannot really harmonize a difficult problem passage with the general teaching of Scripture. In such a case we must wait in faith for a better answer.

Predestination

The word *proorizo,* translated "predestine," means to set or mark off beforehand. Paul told the Ephesian Christians they, as well as he, had been "predestined . . . to adoption as sons through Jesus Christ to Himself, according to the kind intention of His will" (Eph. 1:5). He also said to the same people that they and he had "been predestined according to His purpose who works all things after the counsel of His will" (v. 11 NASB). To the Roman believers the apostle said that all whom God foreknew "He also predestined to become conformed to the image of His Son" (Rom. 8:29).

Charles C. Ryrie's summary of the biblical usage of predestination is true to the text of Scripture.

> Biblically, predestination is limited to the elect people and assures their present position and future destiny. Theologically, the term has been used to include all things, that is, as a synonym for the total plan of God. From this theological definition it is an easy step for some forms of Calvinism to use predestination in relation to the destiny of the nonelect. Thus there arises a doctrine of double predestination. However, this is a logical assumption, not based on biblical texts. The Bible is clear that the elect are predestined, but it never suggests that

there is a similar decree to elect some to damnation. The Scriptures seem content to leave that matter as a mystery, and so should we.[5]

Double Predestination

As indicated in the quotation above, double predestination is a view held by some forms of Calvinism; it is based on the theological use of the term *predestination*. *Double predestination* describes the belief that God predetermined the damnation of some in the same sense in which He chose some to salvation. That is, in both cases He issued a decree—one to save and one to damn. In Scripture, however, the term *predestinate* is always and only used in connection with those who receive God's gift of grace, the elect. It is never used of the nonelect.

Each of the three passages will now be discussed in the order in which they appear in the New Testament.

Romans 9:13

"Just as it is written, 'JACOB I LOVED, BUT ESAU I HATED'" (Rom. 9:13).

Without doubt, Romans 9:13 is one of the most difficult phrases in all the Bible to understand. What could it possibly mean for God to hate Esau in view of the fact that hundreds of times in the Bible we are told God loves all the world?

First, we must be sure to understand the context in which Paul used this problem statement recorded in Malachi 1:1–2. Beginning in Romans 9, the apostle sought to show how the sovereign God works in His dealings with mankind. The nation Israel is used to show how, according to God's own will and sovereign grace, He brings to Himself those who do not deserve His grace. Further, Paul is demonstrating here the abiding faithfulness of God in spite of the disobedience of many Israelites, including Israel's leaders. God would keep His promises to His people. The entire nation was not promised salvation but only those who truly believed.

Kenneth Wuest put it this way:

> It is necessary to keep the apostle's purpose in view. He wishes to show that God's promise has not broken down, though many children of Abraham have no part in its fulfillment in Christ. He does so by showing there has always been a distinction

---

5. Charles C. Ryrie, *Basic Theology* (USA: Victor Books, 1987), 313.

among the descendants of the patriarchs, between those who have merely the natural connection to boast of, and those who are the Israel of God; and, as against Jewish pretensions, he shows at the same time that this distinction can be traced to nothing but God's sovereignty.[6]

The hatred here might be described as "the holy displeasure of God." It must not be compared with the vitriolic animosity often expressed by humans in their relations to others. God is described throughout Scripture as absolutely holy, righteous, and good. No degree of contempt and hatred, as we know it and have perhaps on occasion been guilty of possessing, can be assigned to the God of the Bible.

Perhaps it will be helpful in our understanding of Romans 9:13 to note some other New Testament usages of love and hate. This will help us see how these terms were understood and often used in the culture of New Testament times.

Matthew 10:37

"He who loves father or mother more than Me is not worthy of Me; and he who loves son or daughter more than Me is not worthy of Me" (Matt. 10:37 NASB).

This affirmation from Jesus was given as He was instructing His twelve disciples about the high cost of discipleship. He had already instructed them, "Do not go in the way of the Gentiles, and do not enter any city of the Samaritans; but rather go to the lost sheep of the house of Israel" (Matt. 10:5–6). They also were given instruction concerning what they should take with them and how they should respond to rejection. Jesus told these men they would be hated by all and persecuted. He assured them that He had not come "to bring peace on the earth . . . but a sword" (v. 34). Part of His explanation of what He meant by that was to tell them about the high cost of being worthy of Him, of being His disciple.

In His statement about a disciple loving Him more than his father or mother, Jesus was putting stress on the priority of love for Him. He called for true loyalty of His followers. Jesus was setting forth a comparison between one's love and loyalty for family and an even higher degree of love and loyalty for Him.

---

6. Kenneth Wuest, *Romans in the Greek New Testament* (Grand Rapids: Wm. B. Eerdmans Publishing Company, 1955), 160.

Luke 14:26

"If anyone comes to Me, and does not hate his own father and mother and wife and children and brothers and sisters, yes, and even his own life, he cannot be My disciple" (Luke 14:26 NASB).

Luke's statement about the same saying of Jesus is put in harsher terms. Instead of the *comparative* statement that Matthew gave, Luke set forth a *contrast* statement. We can see from this that Luke's love and hate meant the same as Matthew's loving more and less.

> Discipleship means giving one's first loyalty. There is no place in Jesus' teaching for literal hatred. He commanded His followers to love even their enemies ([Luke] 6:27), so it is impossible to hold that He is here telling them literally to hate their earthly nearest (cf. 8:20f.). But hating can mean something less (Gn. 29:31, 33; Dt. 21:15, where the Hebrew means "hated" and not "disliked," as RSV). Jesus' meaning is surely that the love the disciple has for Him must be so great that the best of earthly loves is hatred by comparison (cf. Mt. 10:37).[7]

John 12:25

"He who loves his life loses it, and he who hates his life in this world will keep it to life eternal" (John 12:25 NASB).

Here is another restatement of the same teaching we found in Matthew 10:37 and Luke 14:26. Jesus had just given the analogy of the grain of wheat dying before it can bear fruit (John 12:24). This illustrated the need for His own death before He would be glorified. The principle illustrated here is that death is the way to life. Our Lord's death led to glory for Himself and for all who believe in Him.

Christ's disciple, Jesus said, must hate his life. In this context and culture, that meant he must be totally Christ-centered and not self-centered. If the disciple puts himself first, an idol has been erected.

Romans 9:22

"What if God, although willing to demonstrate His wrath and to make His power known, endured with much patience vessels of wrath prepared for destruction?" (Rom. 9:22 NASB).

Some Calvinists insist this verse teaches unmistakably that God pre-

---

7. Leon Morris, *The Gospel According to St. Luke* (Grand Rapids: Wm. B. Eerdmans Publishing Company, 1974), 135-36.

destined some to damnation. Does it really do that? Is that the only way to understand what Paul said here? I think not.

The word translated "prepared" is from *katartizō*. In this text it means adjusted, equipped, ripe, ready for "destruction." The passive participle form indicates a present state formed previously. No statement is made as to how this preparation was made. The word *proorizō*, "predestined," is not used in Romans 9:22.

Interestingly, Paul speaks of the elect in Romans 9:23 as "vessels of mercy." This is in contrast to the nonelect as "vessels of wrath" (v. 22). The "vessels of mercy," Paul says, were previously "prepared" for glory (v. 23). Here the word translated "prepared" is from *proetoimazō*. Vincent's discussion of the relation between these two terms is enlightening.

> The studied difference in the use of this term, instead of *katartizō*, to fit Rom. 9:22 cannot be overlooked. The verb is not equivalent to *foreordained* (*proorizō*). *Fitted*, by the adjustment of parts, emphasizes the concurrence of all the elements of the case to the final result. *Prepared* is more general. In the former case the *result* is indicated; in the latter, *the previousness*. Note *before* prepared, while *before* is wanting in verse 22. In this passage the direct agency of God is distinctly stated, in the other, the agency is left indefinite. Here *a single* act is indicated; there *a process*.[8]

1 Peter 2:7–8

"This precious value, then, is for you who believe, but for those who disbelieve, 'THE STONE WHICH THE BUILDERS REJECTED, THIS BECAME THE VERY CORNER *stone*,' and, 'A STONE OF STUMBLING AND A ROCK OF OFFENSE'; for they stumble because they are disobedient to the word, and to this *doom* they were also appointed" (1 Peter 2:7–8 NASB).

This is another biblical text to which those who believe in double predestination turn for support. Does the passage in fact say that God predestined some to damnation?

Peter exhorted his readers to "long for the pure milk of the word, so that by it you may grow in respect to salvation" (1 Peter 2:2). He viewed them as "living stones" (v. 5) and Christ the Lord as a "living stone"

---

8. Marvin R. Vincent, *Word Studies in the New Testament* (Grand Rapids: Wm. B. Eerdmans Publishing Company, 1946), quoted in Wuest, op. cit., 167.

(v. 4) by which they could be built up. Peter then quoted Isaiah 28:16 and Psalm 118:22 to show how the Old Testament anticipated the coming of Christ and a twofold response to Him. Christ, he said, was to those who believe, a "precious value" (1 Peter 2:7) but to those who disbelieve "a stone of stumbling and a rock of offense" (1 Peter 2:8), referring to Isaiah 8:14.

Peter then added the troublesome phrase, that those who stumble over Christ the Lord do so "because they are disobedient to the word, and to this doom they were also appointed" (1 Peter 2:8). To find support from this phrase for predestination to hell, one must find Peter saying that the disobedience or disbelieving is what was ordained of God. But that is not what the text says. Rather, what was ordained for the disbelieving was the penalty of divine judgment.[9] Alan M. Stibbs gave the true meaning of the phrase in 1 Peter 2:8 that is used to support the predestination of people to hell.

> Just as true faith manifests itself in obedience, so heart unbelief inevitably finds expression in deliberate disobedience. In this pathway the disobedient, once they thus set themselves against Christ, find that the Christ who had offered to be for them is against them, interrupting their progress. Such outworking of judgment on unbelief is as divinely appointed as the way of salvation through faith in the exalted Christ.[10]

---

9. Archibald Thomas Robertson, *Word Pictures in the New Testament*, Vol. VI (Nashville: Broadman Press, 1933), 98.

10. Alan M. Stibbs, *The First Epistle General of Peter* (Grand Rapids: Wm. B. Eerdmans Publishing Company, 1974), 103.

Appendix C

A CRITIQUE OF THE MACARTHUR STUDY BIBLE

In recent years there has been renewed emphasis on the view that Christ died only for the elect. Whatever the reason for this reemphasis, God's people need more than ever to know what the Bible says about this important subject. One well-known proponent of the theology of a "limited" atonement recently published a study Bible that likely will become very popular, so an overview of its teaching is in order in this new edition of *The Death Christ Died.*

To my knowledge, John MacArthur's *The MacArthur Study Bible*[11] is the first in the recent crop of study Bibles to strongly advocate the limited view of the atonement. MacArthur has taught this view for a long time in his extensive tape ministry as well as in his writings. His view is particularly evident in discussions of such key passages as Isaiah 53:6; 2 Corinthians 5:14; 5:18–21; Galatians 3:13; 1 Timothy 2:6; 4:10; 1 Peter 2:24; and 1 John 2:2.[12]

---

11. John MacArthur, *The MacArthur Study Bible* (Nashville: Word, 1997).
12. See George Zeller's "The MacArthur Study Bible A Critique," a self-published study available from Middletown Bible Church, 349 East Street, Middletown, CT 06457. This work also sets forth MacArthur's denial of other key doctrines, evidenced in his notes.

Four texts will illustrate MacArthur's view. In each case, I will quote the passage from the New King James Version, the text used in *The MacArthur Study Bible*. This will be followed by selected portions from the study Bible's corresponding notes. I will then compare these comments with the statements of Scripture as normally understood in their historical and contextual sense and the discussion of these texts elsewhere in this book.

1 Timothy 2:5–6

> For *there is* one God and one Mediator between God and men, *the* Man Christ *Jesus who gave Himself a ransom for all*, to be testified in due time. (italics added)

The MacArthur Study Bible *comment:*

> **for all**. This should be taken in two senses: 1) there are temporal benefits of the atonement that accrue to all men universally . . . and 2) Christ's death was sufficient to cover the sins of all people. Yet the substitutionary aspect of His death is applied to the elect alone.[13]

Response to the comment:

Why is there such a narrow definition of "for all," rather than its normal sense of all of Adam's race? MacArthur himself understands Romans 3:23—"All have sinned and fall short of the glory of God"—in this normative way. He, along with other evangelical Christians who believe in limited atonement, take this "all" to refer to every member of Adam's race. There is nothing in the context of 1 Timothy 2:5–6 to warrant restricting "all" to the "elect."

Further, there is nothing in the passage about "temporal benefits" or about Christ's death being "unlimited in its sufficiency but limited in its application." The issue is: *For whom did Christ give Himself a "ransom"*? Commenting on the word *ransom* in the verse, MacArthur correctly states that it "describes the result of Christ's substitutionary death," but then adds the restriction "for believers." Such an interpretation seems unwarranted. See the discussion of 1 Timothy 2:5–6 on pages 24–25.

---

13. MacArthur, *Study Bible,*1683.

Hebrews 2:9

But we see Jesus, who was made a little lower than the angels, for the suffering of death crowned with glory and honor, *that He, by the grace of God, might taste death for everyone.* (italics added)

The MacArthur Study Bible *comment:*

taste death for everyone. Everyone who believes, that is. The death of Christ can only be applied in its efficacy to those who come to God repentantly in faith, asking for saving grace and forgiveness of sins.[14]

Response to the comment:
If the writer of Hebrews meant what MacArthur says he meant, why did he not say so? What MacArthur says here about the efficacy of the death of Christ being applied to those who respond in faith is true. But this statement does not reflect the text's statement "taste death for everyone." There simply are no limitations expressed in the verse. Neither does the verse say anything about the application of the finished work of Christ. The notes do not explain what the text says but rather what MacArthur believes about the extent of the atonement.

2 Peter 2:1

But there were also false prophets among the people, even as there will be false teachers among you, who will secretly bring in destructive heresies, even *denying the Lord who bought them,* and bring on themselves swift destruction. (italics added)

The MacArthur Study Bible *comment:*

who bought them. The terms which Peter used here are more analogical than theological, speaking of a human master over a household. The master bought slaves, and the slaves owed the master allegiance as their sovereign (for an OT parallel, see

14. Ibid., 1899.

Deut. 32:5, 6, where God is said to have bought Israel, though they rejected Him). Doctrinally, this analogy can be viewed as responsibility for submission to God, which the false teachers had refused. Beyond this, they are probably claiming that they were Christians, so that the Lord had bought them actually and personally. With some sarcasm, Peter mocks such a claim by writing of their coming damnation. Thus, the passage is describing the sinister character of the false teachers who claim Christ but deny His lordship over their lives.[15]

Response to the comment:

The context makes it clear that Peter is telling his readers that Christ paid the price of redemption even for those who deny Christ the Lord and will experience certain judgment. Compare this with MacArthur's explanation above. See the discussion of 2 Peter 2:1 on pages 74–75.

1 John 2:1–2

My little children, these things I write to you, that you may not sin. And if anyone sins, we have an Advocate with the Father, Jesus Christ the righteous. And He Himself is the propitiation for our sins, and not for ours only but also *for the whole world.* (italics added)

The MacArthur Study Bible *comment:*

for the whole world. This is a generic term, referring not to every single individual, but to mankind in general. Christ actually paid the penalty only for those who would repent and believe. A number of Scriptures indicate that Christ died for the world (John 1:29; 3:16; 6:51; 1 Tim. 2:6; Heb. 2:9). Most of the world will be eternally condemned to hell to pay for their own sins, so they could not have been paid for by Christ. The passages which speak of Christ's dying for the whole world must be understood to refer to mankind in general (as in Titus 2:3, 4). "World" indicates the sphere, the beings toward whom God seeks reconciliation and has provided propitiation. God has

---

15. Ibid., 1955.

mitigated His wrath on sinners temporarily, by letting them live and enjoy earthly life. . . . In that sense, Christ has provided a brief, temporal propitiation for the whole world. But He actually satisfied fully the wrath of God eternally only for the elect who believe. Christ's death in itself had unlimited and infinite value because He is Holy God. Thus His sacrifice was sufficient to pay the penalty for all the sins of all whom God brings to faith. But the actual satisfaction and atonement was made only for those who believe (cf. John 10:11, 15; 17:9, 20; Acts 20:28; Rom. 8:32, 37; Eph. 5:25). The pardon for sin is offered to the whole world, but received only by those who believe (cf. 4:9, 14; John 5:24). There is no other way to be reconciled to God.[16]

Response to the comment:

Why is "for the whole world" a "generic term, referring not to every single individual, but to mankind in general"? What in this verse allows one to say, "Christ actually paid the penalty only for those who would repent and believe"? Again, MacArthur insists on omitting reference to the fact that *world* often does refer to every member of Adam's lost race—the inhabited world. On what basis does he restrict the term's meaning here? Is there something in the context which makes it obvious that the whole world is not intended here? No such limitation can be supported from the immediate or remote context of the passage. All those who believe in limited atonement bring the limitation to the passage. In other words, their theology dictates to them what the passage must say. See the discussion of 1 John 2:1–2 on pages 81–85.

When respected and popular evangelical Bible teachers such as John MacArthur advocate that Christ did not die for every member of Adam's race, the need arises for the restatement of the historic biblical view that, in fact, He did die as a substitute for all without exception. Along with this need, there also comes the urgency to remind all that Christ's substitutionary death was a provision for salvation. The debt of sin has been paid in full. Salvation is now offered to all who will receive the gift by faith alone in Christ alone.

---

16. Ibid., 1965.

BIBLIOGRAPHY

Douty, Norman F. *The Death of Christ*. Swengel, Penn.: Reiner, 1972.

McCarthy, James G. *The Gospel According to Rome: Comparing Catholic Tradition and the Word of God*. Eugene, Ore.: Harvest House, 1995.

Zeller, George. *For Whom Did Christ Die? A Defense of Unlimited Atonement*. A study published by Middletown Bible Church, Middletown, Conn.

SCRIPTURE INDEX